MAO

IN THE BOARDROOM

Marketing Genius
from the Mind of the
Master Guerrilla

MAO

IN THE BOARDROOM

Gabriel Stricker

St. Martin's Griffin ⋈ New York

www.stmartins.com

Design by Ralph L. Fowler

Grateful acknowledgment is made for use of material from
On Guerilla Warfare by Mao Tse-tung, translated by Samuel B.
Griffith II. Copyright © 1961 by Samuel B. Griffith. Reprinted with
permission of Jane Griffith and Belle Gordon Griffith Heneberger.

All original photographs on pages headed "The Chairman Speaks"
reprinted by permission of Getty Images; alterations by the author.

All other photographs in the book reprinted by permission of AP/Wide
World Photos with alterations by the author.

Library of Congress Cataloging-in-Publication Data
Stricker, Gabriel.
    Mao in the boardroom : marketing genius from the mind of
    the master guerrilla / Gabriel Stricker.
       p. cm.
    ISBN 0-312-31085-4
    1. Marketing. 2. Marketing executives. I. Title.
HF5415.S86995 2003
658.8—dc21   2002045244

10 9 8 7 6 5 4 3

Well my telephone was ringing and
they told me it was Chairman Mao
You got to tell him anything 'cause
I just don't want to talk to him now

—"Apolitical Blues," by Lowell George

Contents

Introduction

guer·ril·la \gə-'ri-lə\ *n.* (1809) **1:** a member of an irregular, independent band of soldiers operating in occupied territory to harass and undermine the enemy, as by surprise raids, attacks on communication and supply lines.

mar·ket·ing \mär-ki-tĭng\ *n.* (1561) **1:** the act or process of selling or purchasing in a market.

cam·paign \kam-'pān\ *n.* (1652) **1:** a connected series of military operations forming a distinct phase of a war.

Move over, Steve Jobs. Move over, Ben and Jerry. Step aside, Richard Branson and Vince McMahon. You think you were the first guerrilla marketers? Mao—the original "Chairman" of the board—beat you to the punch years ago.

Mao may not have been a capitalist at heart, but he sure knew how to wage an underdog war against a better armed, better equipped, Goliath opponent. And he knew how to win.

Mao Tse-tung wrote *On Guerrilla Warfare* in 1937,[1] while China was in the throes of Japanese occupation. He derived the core principles of *On Guerrilla Warfare* from Sun-tzu's *The Art of War*. Mao studied *The Art of War* and put many of its theories into action during more than a decade of personal experience in the trenches.

> **Mao may not have been a capitalist at heart, but he sure knew how to wage an underdog war against a better armed, better equipped, Goliath opponent. And he knew how to win.**

Faced with a Japanese army of superior strength, Mao realized that Sun-tzu's principles of conventional warfare were no longer sufficient. In response, *On Guerrilla Warfare* was more than just a short, ten thousand-word how-to guide for guerrilla fighting. It was a message to the citizens of China—and the rest of the world—that the rules of engagement had changed. Forever.

Fast-forward more than a half century from the highlands of Hunan and the surroundings of Szechwan to the boardrooms of America. Mao's disciples abound. RCN takes on AOL Time Warner. Oakley outflanks Ray Ban. Skyy Vodka subverts Stoli. And *Maxim* magazine marauds the marketplace.

These are the guerrillas of our time, born in the tradition of Mao, but unleashed on capitalism with a fury. How did they do it? How do they continue to do it? How can these corporate Davids continually hit industry Goliaths right between the eyes? By applying the principles of Mao's *On Guerrilla Warfare* in their everyday battles against a better armed, better equipped opponent. Like any good guerrilla, they overcome a bigger, badder rival with smarter strategy.

Mao's *On Guerrilla Warfare* was designed for the battlefield, but it is just as useful in the boardroom.

PART ONE

Guerrilla Companies

The Chairman speaks:

"I-P-Oh. I-P-Ohhh. I-P-Ohhhhhhh."

CHAPTER 1

Guerrilla Warfare Defined

Changing the Rules

The Chairman speaks:

"We're Mao, Hahn, Bell, Larkin, Yarbrough and Associates. What the hell are *you* looking at?!"

MAO

Guerrilla Warfare Defined

"What is basic guerrilla strategy? Guerrilla strategy must be based primarily on alertness, mobility, and attack. It must be adjusted to the enemy situation, the terrain, the existing lines of communication, the relative strengths, the weather and the situation of the people.

As to the matter of . . . responsibilities, those of the guerrillas are to exterminate small forces of the enemy; to harass and weaken large forces; to attack enemy lines of communications; to establish bases capable of supporting independent operations . . . to force the enemy to disperse his strength . . . "

—Mao Tse-tung

Guerrilla Warfare Defined

Only the strongest survive, right?

Wrong.

Guerrillas don't play by those rules. In guerrilla warfare, only the *smartest* survive.

Guerrillas acknowledge the existence of the old rules—of "their" rules—and then break them.

Guerrillas look at the competitive landscape with a beginner's mind.

- **Skyy** demands that we evaluate vodka on its purity.

- **Apple** mandates that everyone Think Different.

- And **Swatch** orders us to look at watches as anything but timepieces.

Get ready, the guerrillas are coming. If you're waging a conventional war, beware, lest you be left in the dust.

Their Rules: Only the strongest survive.

Our Rules: Only the smartest survive.

IN THE BOARDROOM

Skyy: "Clean Vodka" Is Not an Oxymoron

Maurice Kanbar spent his entire life changing the game. Before starting Skyy Vodka, Kanbar, who says he's "rather inquisitive,"[2] brought the world the "D-fuzz-it"—a device that removes fluff balls from wool sweaters. He invented a piece of equipment to hold incisions open during operations. He invented a gadget that gets rid of varicose veins. He even invented a device that removes cataracts from eyes. And in case that wasn't enough, Kanbar is also credited with inventing the first-ever multiplex movie theater.[3]

All told, Kanbar holds patents on more than 30 products. Skyy Vodka is among them.

Changing the Rules

Skyy Vodka is unique not only because of its cobalt-blue bottle. It is unique because it is a product that succeeded in changing the rules even after the rules had already been changed.

Absolut Vodka was the first to change the rules. It was the first vodka that refused to compete over the level of "Russianness" it contained. Absolut was Swedish and proud of it. Absolut refused to play the Russian-vodka game.

Kanbar and Skyy changed the rules again by insisting that vodka be about purity and quality. At the time, Skyy's introduction of purity into how vodkas should be evaluated was groundbreaking. Vodka, after all, was the drink of Siberia. It was about boldness and punch. It had the purity of an automobile crankshaft. And that was okay.

> **Skyy's introduction of purity into how vodkas should be evaluated was groundbreaking. Vodka, after all, had the purity of an automobile crankshaft. And that was okay.**

It was okay until Maurice Kanbar had a headache one morning. "It may sound obvious, but things are only ever invented because they're needed, and I needed something that wouldn't give me a headache." Kanbar and a physician friend quickly went to work and discovered that headaches were caused by a sensitivity to "congeners"—the natural impurities formed in alcohol during the fermentation process.[4]

After a year of tinkering, Kanbar developed Skyy—"the smoothest, cleanest, purest vodka imaginable."

Mao was there.

"I still drink Stoli sometimes," said Mao. "But when you want a killer martini, you've gotta have Skyy."

He finally found a manufacturer in Germany that would attempt his complicated quadruple distillation and triple filtration processes—and then put it all together in striking blue bottles.

Hangover-free (for a while at least)

Initially, Skyy staked its claim as a vodka so pure that it was "hangover-free." Following pressure from the U.S. Bureau of Alcohol, Tobacco and Firearms, Skyy decided to drop its claim.[5] "It's not our intention to deceive anyone in any way," Kanbar said at the time. "There's no question that some may feel this is just a marketing gimmick. These are the same guys that can drink kerosene and not get a headache."[6]

But despite having to back down from its original positioning, Skyy had *already* won. Skyy had changed the rules—even before the rule-makers had a chance to intervene. "Congener" may not have become a permanent entry in the drinking lexicon. But the word *sky* with an extra *y* definitely has.

Apple: Computers for People Who Can't Program Their VCRs

"Most of the people running the companies don't love PCs. Does [Microsoft CEO] Steve Ballmer love PCs? Does [Intel CEO] Craig Barrett love PCs? Does Michael Dell love PCs? If he wasn't selling PCs he'd be selling something else! We have this incredible, unshakable belief that if we make the coolest computers, make them more affordable, more powerful, then we're going to be successful."[7]

The three pioneers of Silicon Valley: Jobs, Mao, Wozniak. Mao was instrumental in Apple's shift toward the Macintosh platform. "The people love a mouse," he said.

Mao was there.

Mao initially took offense to Apple's 1984 Super Bowl ad. "Must you portray totalitarianism in such *bad* light?" he asked Steve Jobs.

Such are the musings of one of the original guerrillas of Silicon Valley: Apple's Steve Jobs.

Apple and Orwell

Jobs was responsible for one of the loudest guerrilla "shots" heard around the world. On January 22, 1984, during the third quarter of the Super Bowl, Apple aired a sixty-second commercial. The spot was directed by Ridley Scott, and reportedly cost $400,000—an astronomical figure at the time. It aired only once.[8]

The commercial depicted an Orwellian scene where a heroic woman donning a Macintosh tank top hurls a hammer into the big brother of IBM, interrupting his dictatorial speech: "A garden of pure ideology where each worker may bloom, secure from the pests. . . . We are one people with one whim, one resolve. . . . We shall prevail!" The ad concludes with, "On January twenty-fourth Apple Computer will introduce Macintosh. And you'll see why 1984 won't be like *1984*."

At the time, Jobs described the Macintosh as "the last force for freedom" in the marketplace.[9]

In the years that followed, Apple experienced tremendous turbulence—at one point leading to Jobs being ousted in a coup by then-CEO/"corporate anti-hero" John Sculley.[10] But Jobs and Apple both came back—literally and figuratively.

Comrade Jobs Returns

By 1996, Jobs had returned to Apple's trenches. His mission was to once again make a difference—"and not just for his own gratification, but for the sake of 'the rest of us,' as he put it."[11] By "the rest of us," Jobs meant those individuals who could not—and would not—tolerate technological devices any more complicated than a standard AM/FM car radio. "The rest of us" didn't know how to program a VCR. "The rest of us" did not know what a RAM or a CPU was. "The rest of us" did not enjoy using computers.

> **Jobs' mission was to make a difference for "the rest of us"— those individuals who could not program a VCR and did not know what a RAM or a CPU was. "The rest of us" did not enjoy using computers.**

In May of 1998, Apple released the iMac—the company's gift to "the rest of us." The iMac featured a stylish new case design, with translucent plastics in new trailblazing colors—"Bondi Blue," "Strawberry," "Blueberry," "Tangerine," "Lime," and "Grape." It

A soon-to-be-released version of Apple's now-legendary ad campaign.

had a simple pocket-sized user's manual. And it came with a mandate from the company: "Think different."

"Here's to the crazy ones," Apple said in its original "Think different" commercial. "We make tools for these kinds of people. While some see them as the crazy ones, we see genius. Because the people who are crazy enough to think they can change the world, are the ones who do." Apple had done it again. Guerrilla resurrection.

For Every Season: Swatch, Swatch, Swatch

The Swiss call him the "Uhrenkonig" or "Watch King."[12] His name is Nicolas Hayek, and nearly two decades ago, he had a truly radical idea for revolutionizing the watch industry.

Watches are for status. Wrong. Watches are heirlooms. Nope. Watches are for timekeeping. Not so.

Watches, Hayek decreed, are for *fashion*.

Enter Swatch.

"When Swatch came with the idea of having a very high-quality Swiss watch that was a provocation and had a joyful approach, we changed the way people used watches," says Hayek.

"In the past, people would keep a watch for twenty years or so," Hayek remembers. "And then Swatch

> **Watches are for status. Wrong. Watches are heirlooms. Nope. Watches are for timekeeping. Not so. Watches, Swatch's Nicolas Hayek decreed, are for *fashion*.**

came and nobody says, 'When I get the watch I'll keep it for my life.' You keep it, you like it. You see another one, you buy it; you have another one for sport, you change it. Today it is totally normal."[13]

A Watch for Every Limb

To emphasize Swatch's fashion-watch paradigm, Hayek wears two watches, "one set at Swiss time, the other set for local time. Both, naturally, are Swatches." He explains, "It's a tradition in the house that most of the Swatch people are wearing two watches. It's like working in a chocolate company, you eat chocolate."[14]

With its reliable, high-quality, slim, plastic-bodied, battery-powered, fifty-one-component, quartz-movement watches—many of which priced at a highly affordable $40 or less—Swatch has single-handedly taken the Swiss share of the world watch market from 15 percent in 1983 to more than 50 percent today.[15] "My whole life has been spent swimming against the tide," Hayek says. "When we launched the Swatch everybody said we would never sell more than a hundred thousand."[16] Today, over 250 million units later, it is the most successful wristwatch of all time.[17]

A key gear in Swatch's successful business machine has been its ability to stay fresh and original.

Mao was there.

Mao and Swatch's Nicolas Hayek. "I was actually the first to start the two-watch craze," said Mao. "You can never be too punctual in today's fast-paced world."

Swatch launches almost three hundred new designs every year, with special models for every season . . . and every reason.[18] Since 1983, nearly four thousand different designs have been created—including butterfly and zebra Swatches, Yoko Ono and Keith Haring Swatches, Che Guevara and James Bond Swatches, and on and on.

"Always new, always different," pronounces Swatch's motto.[19] It is a philosophy Swatch has carried from the start—ever since it stopped time and started fashion—all in one fell swoop. Tick-tock chic.

CHAPTER 2 **War Defined**

The Chairman speaks:

"I'm Mao. This is Mr. Dow. We're here to pump . . .
you up."

War Defined

" Before we treat the practical aspects of guerrilla war, it might be well to recall the fundamental axiom of combat on which all military action is based. This can be stated: 'Conservation of one's own strength; destruction of enemy strength.' "

—Mao Tse-tung

War Defined

The boardroom is the war room. It is the place where we contemplate how to realize victory and how to avoid defeat.

Business, as it has been said time and time again, is war. It is a fight, as Mao says, to conserve our strengths and destroy the enemy's strengths.

When we adopt a business-war mentality, it prevents us from becoming complacent. It keeps us on our toes. It forces us to always keep our eyes open—vigilant over our competitors' every move.

Business may be enjoyable. It may be downright fun sometimes.

But we must always remember that it is most certainly a war, and at all times there are those who would like to eliminate us, just as we would like to eliminate them.

Just take a look at **HBO** in its battle against the network television establishment, and **Oakley,** where

IN THE BOARDROOM

the home of sunglasses is in a permanent state of DEFCON 1.

Their Rules: *Fight and then take it easy.*

Our Rules: *Fight and then maintain the red alert at all times.*

HBO: Putting the Networks Six Feet Under

It's Not TV. It's HBO. . . . And It's War

Over the past 30 years, Home Box Office (HBO) has quietly and scrappily clawed its way into its current position as the single most prestigious television network in the United States.[20] Since its beginning, HBO has built a business defining itself as the anti-network, but its war against the television establishment finally reached its peak in the mid-90s with five simple words: "It's not TV. It's HBO." *Cable World's* Verne Gay teased apart the meaning of HBO's motto as follows: "TV isn't any good at all, but because we aren't TV, we are good. . . . We don't have any witless sitcoms or clueless dramas or lousy made-for-TV movies . . . And, while we're at it, we don't have any commercials either, which are really a pain in the ass, aren't they?"[21] Ann Thomopoulos, senior vice president of original programming, explained HBO's war cry in gentler terms: "The stories we attack are slightly different. They lend themselves to more original thinking."[22]

The Counterprogramming Revolution

With "It's not TV. It's HBO." as its fight song, HBO intensified its fierce battle against broadcast network

Goliaths CBS, NBC, ABC, and increasingly, Fox. Like all smart guerrilla organizations, HBO fought the networks with rules that were stacked in its own favor. At the center of HBO's rules was "counterprogramming" — the system of producing shows that the established broadcast networks would not or (because of laws reg-

> "TV isn't any good at all, but because we aren't TV, we are good. . . . We don't have any witless sitcoms or clueless dramas or lousy made-for-TV movies . . . And, while we're at it, we don't have any commercials either, which are really a pain in the ass, aren't they?"

ulating programming content) *could not* produce. "We look for provocative and interesting stuff wherever we can find it," explained Carolyn Strauss, executive vice president of original programming.[23] "Because [the broadcast networks] have a volume requirement, once they find something that works, they try to turn it into a formula," added Thomopoulos. "We consciously try to avoid formula. When an audience starts to feel they anticipate your next move, it's less satisfying."[24]

HBO's avoidance of a predictable formula and its adherence to programming that challenges social norms have given rise to a string of highly popular and critically acclaimed series including *Six Feet Under, Sex and the City, Oz, Curb Your Enthusiasm,* and one of the most financially successful television shows of all time, *The Sopranos.*[25] Verne Gay explained HBO's method as follows: "HBO and [Chairman Chris] Albrecht don't bug star producers with the (sometimes) inane and petty demands that occasionally (okay, often) turn commercial TV shows into hackneyed, clichéd piles of mush."[26] *Broadcasting & Cable* magazine added, "While ABC, CBS and NBC are known for barraging writers with script changes and hemming them in with rules (happy endings, blatant story lines, heroes motivated primarily by good), HBO has a reputation for leaving writers alone, except perhaps to coach them on how to break the rules."[27]

The Networks Get Whacked by *The Sopranos*

With *The Sopranos* (initially called *Family Man*[28] and later renamed), HBO has broken the rules while at the same time breaking the spirit of network television programmers. Verne Gay summarized, "*The Sopranos* . . . forced the major commercial networks to ask themselves, 'Why can't we do this?' . . . There are lots of reasons why they can't, and as a result, HBO has in hand a specific example of why it is demonstrably superior to its commercial brethren."[29]

> **At the center of HBO's rules was "counterprogramming"—the system of producing shows that the established broadcast networks would not or (because of laws regulating programming content) could not produce.**

The first-ever *Sopranos* episode in 1999 mustered a meager 7.7 Nielsen Media Research rating points (each rating point represents 1,067,000 households). That number ballooned to 20.4 for the season-three premiere;[30] it is currently the highest-rated cable series of all time.[31] This is particularly impressive considering the fact that HBO can only be seen by its

38 million subscribers; two thirds of homes with television in the United States *do not* receive HBO.

Despite its humble beginnings, *The Sopranos* has fueled subscription growth more than any other single HBO show.[32] Meanwhile, HBO's 2002 earnings were nearly triple their 1995 levels—"north of $800 million"—according to Chairman Albrecht. By comparison, NBC—the most profitable of the broadcast networks—had earnings of just over $500 million for the same period.[33]

Countering Counterinsurgency with Continued Counterprogramming

The broadcast networks' response to HBO's reign of terror has been to counterattack with similarly racy and edgy programming. ABC's *NYPD Blue* generated controversy with frequent scenes of violence and nudity, and an early episode in which a male character called a woman a "bitch." NBC launched the Sopranosesque *Kingpin*—a show chronicling a Mexican drug cartel.[34] HBO is countering network counterinsurgency with continued counterprogramming—this time with toned-*down* shows: *Carnivale,* which follows a band of traveling carneys in the Oklahoma Dust Bowl of 1934, and *Dead Wood,* a Western focusing on a merchant who sets up shop in a pros-

Mao was there.

Mao accepting an Emmy Award for his appearance as the hit man "Chairman Goomba" in *The Sopranos*. "It was a good role for me. At first, I had a hard time figuring out my motivation. Then it all came naturally."

pecting town two weeks after the Battle of the Little Big Horn.[35] Critics are already cheering HBO's latest programming attack and predicting further victory in its television wars. As for the broadcast networks, just when they thought they were out, HBO keeps pulling them back in.

Oakley: All's Fair in Sunglasses and War

To some, sunglasses may seem like a "nice" industry; shades are just a cute accessory, after all. To Oakley, the sunglasses industry is anything but "nice"—Oakley views itself in an ongoing state of war.

From Dogs and Motorcycles to Shades

The roots of this war began in 1965 when Jim Jannard produced specialized motorcycle handlebar grips out of his garage, naming the company "Oakley" after his dog.[36] The war escalated in 1980 when Jannard made a simple realization: When motocross stars are interviewed on television, their heads and faces are highly visible. The company then released goggles with the Oakley name prominently displayed—quickly gaining the company recognition and helping it establish a "reputation for functional quality and unique design."[37]

But the war began in earnest in 1984 when Oakley released its first sunglasses. The war was to be fought against Bausch & Lomb. Against Ray Ban. Later, it would even be fought against Nike.[38]

When Oakley held its first shareholders' meeting in 1996, it did so not at a golf resort or in a conference

> **Oakley held its first shareholders' meeting not at a golf resort or in a conference room, but in an aircraft hangar at the El Toro Marine Corps Air Station in California.**

room. It held its meeting in an aircraft hangar at the El Toro Marine Corps Air Station in California. CEO Mike Parnell explained, "We couldn't see ourselves in a hotel ballroom. We're in a war."[39]

Guerrilla Hideout

Oakley's headquarters in the Southern California foothills "could easily be mistaken for a space-age fortress rather than a corporate headquarters. And with giant breastplates adorning its gates, models of torpedoes and land mines decorating its corridors and B-52 ejector seats passing for furniture, it certainly appears that some kind of war is going on."[40]

The company lays claim to more than six hundred patents and eight hundred trademarks invented in its

Irvine, California, factory—or as the company tells it—"born in the depths of a design bunker."[41] Jamie Oman, product-testing supervisor for Oakley, explains, "Oh yeah. We've got to protect what we've worked so hard to get."[42] At Oakley, the war rages on.

Mao was there.

Every leader must have his sunglasses. Oakley custom designed these "M Shades" for Mao with special lenses that filter out all dissenters.

CHAPTER 3

Even Conventional Organizations Can Use Guerrilla Tactics

The Chairman speaks:

"I really need you guys to think OUT OF THE BOX on this one. Your usual recycled nonsense just won't do this time."

MAO

Even Conventional Organizations Can Use Guerrilla Tactics

> Orthodox forces may under certain conditions operate as guerrillas, and the latter may, under certain conditions, develop to the status of the former.
>
> —Mao Tse-tung

Even Conventional Organizations Can Use Guerrilla Tactics

"Guerrilla" is not a permanent characteristic. It is not as eternal as ethnicity or race. Guerrilla is a state of mind—an attitude. Established, "conventional" organizations can compete with—and ultimately *beat*—upstart guerrillas by adopting the guerrilla mindset.

> **Their Rules:** *We're too big to be guerrillas.*
>
> **Our Rules:** *We're too big not to be.*

Goliaths can stymie the attacks of David not just by continuing to overpower David, but by behaving like David himself.

Think it can't be done? Think Goliaths can't act like Davids? Take a quick look at **AT&T**—the "mother" of all conventional companies.

IN THE BOARDROOM

At&T: Gets Lucky . . . Lucky Dog, That Is

In February 1999, AT&T did something it hadn't done since the company was founded in 1855: It introduced a new brand that did not explicitly mention AT&T by name. Actually, it didn't even mention AT&T *implicitly*. In fact, when AT&T launched the Lucky Dog Phone Company, AT&T wanted absolutely nothing to do with, well, itself.[43]

Lucky Dog doesn't ring a bell? Well perhaps 10-10-345 does.

AT&T's stealthy spin-off was introduced at a time when other similar 10-10 or "dial around" numbers were so popular with consumers that on their own they accounted for a near $2 billion industry.[44] Initially, AT&T dismissed 10-10 service as a passing fad. "We thought it would come and go," said Howard E. McNally, the AT&T executive who ran the Lucky Dog operation. "We understand the market a little bit better now."[45]

MCI, the market leader at the time, was so enthralled by the 10-10 craze that it actually had two numbers for consumers to dial under its spin-off, Telecom USA: 10-10-220 and 10-10-321.

Not to be outdone, WorldxChange had three: 10-10-629, 10-10-275 and 10-10-502.

Mao was there.

Dial and Save!
10-10-345

Mao, an early adopter of "dial around" service, always preferred 10-10-345 over 10-10-321. "How else can you call Peking for ten cents a minute?!" he exclaimed.

There were other players such as VarTec Telecom: 10-10-811.

Or Excel: 10-10-297.

And how could we forget Qwest: 10-10-432?

A company named PT-1 spiced things up a bit with its 10-16-868 service.[46]

And so on.

AT&T had seen enough. It had seen enough, mostly because 10-10 services were costing the telecom giant valuable market share. John Donoghue, then a senior vice president for marketing at MCI WorldCom, said that more than 85 percent of MCI's 10-10-321 users were AT&T customers.[47]

When AT&T launched Lucky Dog, it seemed to suggest an "if you can't beat 'em, join 'em strategy." While Lucky Dog might have appeared to be a tactic by AT&T to *join* a movement, it was, in fact, a tactic to *destroy* a movement.

> **While Lucky Dog might have appeared to be a tactic by AT&T to *join* a movement, it was, in fact, a tactic to *destroy* a movement.**

Clear Consumer Confusion

Consumers, already confused and overwhelmed by the onslaught of 10-10 numbers, were beginning to return to their previous carriers—which, more often than not, was AT&T. Lucky Dog further "confused" consumers back to their traditional carriers. "We thought [MCI's] pricing was very confusing," AT&T's McNally said. "That's why we decided that we'd be very clear."[48] Or clearly confusing.

"If they wreck the category it's still to their advantage," said Brian Adamik, a communications analyst for the Yankee Group, a technology consulting firm in Boston, while adding that, "if they can in some way contribute to the demise of the industry, they win, because they still have the lion's share of the market."[49]

"It gives us a chance to be, in some ways, out of character for AT&T," said Mark Siegel, an AT&T spokesman in Basking Ridge, New Jersey.[50] Yes, in some ways, out of character for AT&T. In other ways, it was just Ma Bell in sheep's clothing.

CHAPTER 4 **Guerrilla Warfare Used in Conjunction with Conventional Warfare**

The Chairman speaks:

"We're all about implementing ACTIONABLE BUSINESS SOLUTIONS at this firm. *That's* why we're unique."

Guerrilla Warfare Used in Conjunction with Conventional Warfare

> These guerrilla operations must not be considered as an independent form of warfare. They are but one step in the total war, one aspect of the revolutionary struggle.
>
> This [guerrilla] warfare must be developed to an unprecedented degree and it must coordinate with the operations of our regular armies. If we fail to do this, we will find it difficult to defeat the enemy.
>
> —Mao Tse-tung

Guerrilla Warfare Used in Conjunction with Conventional Warfare

Unless we monopolized a market (Boeing) or created an altogether new market-category (Kinko's), we were all guerrillas at one time. Guerrilla tactics likely led us into our state of prosperity and stability. We must not forget the scrappy roots from whence we came.

At times, it is essential for established organizations to complement their conventional strategy with guerrilla strategy. Used in tandem, conventional tactics and guerrilla tactics can either overpower other aspiring guerrillas or destroy industry co-competitors.

- **Coca-Cola** complemented its conventional forces with an elite guerrilla team called **Fruitopia** designed to overthrow **Snapple**.

- **Phillip Morris** and **R. J. Reynolds** developed

IN THE BOARDROOM

smaller, elite guerrilla units to carve out new market share.

The Rules: *We look forward to the day when we no longer have to be guerrillas.*

Our Rules: *If there's a day when we're no longer guerrillas, then there will be no tomorrow to look forward to.*

Mao says that experience shows us that guerrilla operations alone "cannot produce final victory." The question for all of you Goliaths out there is, "Got guerrilla?"

Coca-Cola and Fruitopia
Sip from Snapple's Sweet Strategy

"We were street guys—we didn't go to Harvard," said Arnold Greenberg, who, along with childhood buddies Leonard Marsh and Hyman Golden, started Unadulterated Food Products, Inc., which in 1978 became the beverage company Snapple. "We went more with guts. We would buck the market surveys if we didn't think they were right."

The Plain People's Beverage

"What [Greenberg and Marsh] did was really historic," said John Sicher, publisher of *Beverage Digest,* an industry newsletter. "We made the first ready-to-drink iced tea that didn't taste like battery acid," Greenberg explained.[51]

Equally historic, Marsh continued, "We dealt with the plain people of America, that's who we wanted to attract. Of the 260 million people in America, 258 million of them are plain people. I wanted the 258 million to drink Snapple."

Using their grandmother's home cold remedy that added jam to tea,[52] many of the "plain people" started drinking Snapple by the caseload. And many of those plain people drank Snapple instead of other tradi-

> **Through shrewd guerrilla strategy, Snapple had shifted the war from the previous carbonated battlefield to the unknown jungle of noncarbonated fruit- and tea-drinks.**

tional plain-people beverages such as Coca-Cola. Through shrewd guerrilla strategy, Snapple had shifted the war from the previous carbonated battle-field to the unknown jungle of noncarbonated fruit- and tea-drinks.

Coke Goes Guerrilla

By March of 1994, Coke had had enough. It released a line of noncarbonated beverages called Fruitopia—a name that was reportedly coined by two students at Ohio's Miami University during a Coca-Cola–sponsored marketing project.[53]

"We don't want Snapple to be without a competitor," said Coca-Cola's chairman and chief executive,

Roberto C. Goizueta, "so that's why we launched Fruitopia."[54]

Innovation Over Brawn

To get even with Snapple, Coke couldn't simply get mad, it had to get *smart*. "The world's leading soft drink company is using innovation rather than its traditional brawn to overwhelm the competition," wrote Coca-Cola's hometown *Atlanta Journal and Constitution*.[55]

Getting smart came in the form of getting guerrilla. To play catch-up in the "alternative" beverage category, Coca-Cola had to use an "alternative" mindset. "We found consumers want the yin of the new mixed with the yang of the traditional," explained Sergio Zyman, then Coca-Cola's global marketing chief.[56]

Coke's yin was a New Agey, throwback advertising campaign called "Welcome to Fruitopian Life." The effort reinforced Fruitopia's already alternative product names (such as Strawberry Passion Awareness and The Grape Beyond) with offbeat "thoughts" including:

- "Don't judge fruit or people by the color of their skin,"[57]

- "The apples don't fight the pineapples in Fruit Integration," and

- "This is what Citrus Consciousness can do to your tongue, imagine what it can do to your soul."[58]

The public bought it. "Fruitopia snaps up market share with its new identity," said a *USA Today* headline. "Suddenly, Fruitopia's become Snapple's worst nightmare."[59]

Mao was there.

Mao begrudgingly reaches for a Fruitopia after a long day on the road. "I was always partial to Snapple," he said. "But after they were sold to Quaker and then to Triarc and then to Cadbury, I thought, 'What the heck. Might as well go for the one with the cooler name.' "

Fruitopia's Utopic Success

By May of 1998 Fruitopia was outselling Snapple in convenience stores and service station mini-markets. Two years later, Snapple was still the leader of the $2.2 billion industry, with 12.4 percent of the market, but Fruitopia had skyrocketed to 8.5 percent.[60] In just over five years, Coke had entered the guerrilla jungle and nearly leveled the playing field.

"Our purpose is to provide consumers the variety they're looking for and demanding," said Tom Reddin, Coke's director of U.S. consumer marketing for noncarbonated beverages in 1997. "We provide a lot of that with our carbonated soft drinks, but there's also a role for these drinks."[61] Reddin was, in essence, making reference to one of Mao's core strategies: When used in conjunction with traditional warfare (Coke), guerrilla warfare (Fruitopia) can be highly effective.

Philip Morris and R. J. Reynolds Smoke the "Big" Out of Big Tobacco

By 1995, Big Tobacco's name was mud. The "Big" of Big Tobacco was synonymous with "Bad." So what did companies like Philip Morris and R. J. Reynolds do? They went guerrilla—they went small.

For a Big Tobacco company like Philip Morris, you couldn't get much smaller than Dave's Tobacco Company. Stealing a move out of wine industry giant E. & J. Gallo's playbook when they used the fictitious Frank and Ed to sell Bartles & Jaymes, Philip Morris created Dave, "a fictional character" meant to sym-

Bartles, Jaymes and Mao. "Those guys were all right, I guess," said Mao. "But that Frank fella wasn't much of a talker."

bolize "a home-style, homespun campaign with a grass-roots feel," said Karen Daragan, a spokeswoman for Philip Morris USA.[62]

Big Tobacco Goes Small

"Down in Concord, N.C., there's a guy named Dave," starts Dave's Tobacco Company's promotional literature. "He lives in the heart of tobacco farmland.

> The "Big" of Big Tobacco was synonymous with "Bad." So what did companies like Philip Morris and R. J. Reynolds do? They went guerrilla — they went small.

Dave enjoys lots of land, plenty of freedom and his yellow '57 pickup truck. Dave was fed up with cheap, fast-burning smokes. Instead of just getting mad, he did something about it. Dave's tobacco company was born."[63]

The press materials further describe Dave as "an entrepreneur who believes in the value of homemade products and the concept of offering folks quality cigarettes at the right price." Dave tells store owners he doesn't even want his folksy smokes to "mix with the 'corporate' cigarettes."[64]

> **Humor columnist Dave Barry explained, "The people at Philip Morris are just calling the new brand 'Dave's' because ... Dave is easy to spell and easy to say when you're lying on the floor drunk."**

Another Dave—syndicated humor columnist Dave Barry—explained, "The people at Philip Morris are just calling the new brand 'Dave's' because they think the name 'Dave' sounds trustworthy and noncorporate. This is pretty funny when you consider that Philip Morris is the world's largest tobacco company and has enough marketing experts and advertising consultants and lawyers and lobbyists to sink an aircraft carrier, not that I'm suggesting anything."[65] He added that the choice of the name "Dave" was a good

Mao was there.

Mao trying out a Dave's Tobacco Company smoke (Philip Morris' foray into the micro-cig category) for the first time. "Tastes like a Marlboro," he said.

one since "Dave is easy to spell and easy to say when you're lying on the floor drunk."[66]

But Big Tobacco's guerrilla efforts were not simply a move to seem more "trustworthy and noncorporate." They were also driven by an emerging trend in the tobacco industry, where upstarts such as the Santa Fe Natural Tobacco Company's "American Spirit," an all-natural product launched in 1983, were enjoying increased sales and were even being sold in some health-food stores. Financial figures from 1999 indicate that American Spirit's sales topped $75 million,[67] and by 2002, R. J. Reynolds Tobacco had to raise the white flag by buying Santa Fe Natural Tobacco Company, Inc. for $340 million in cash.[68] This came in the aftermath of RJR's own attempt at counterinsurgency.

RJR Can Play Small Too

In 1995, R. J. Reynolds Tobacco launched the Moonlight Tobacco Company—a "unique division operated as an independent entity." Moonlight offered over a dozen separate products including:

- **Jumbos** with an elephant promoting its wide-gauge cigarettes,

- **Politix** with what could be mistaken as an election poster for Richard Nixon, described as "retro political symbology,"

- **Fedora** whose felt hat icon "evokes the brand's smooth, mellow, sophisticated taste and style,"

- **Icebox** that includes "the charm of an old-fashioned icebox and a snowflake illustration to impart the menthol cooling sensation of the brand," as well as

- **North Star** with packaging that "suggests Eastern European military imagery."[69]

"It's for folks who have much more of an alternative, free-spirited lifestyle," explained Cliff Pennell, RJR's senior vice president for brands. "They don't like the mass or the mainstream. They like to be dif-

Mao was there.

Here, Mao is pictured smoking a "North Star" cigarette—one of Moonlight Tobacco's numerous brands. "I know it's an RJR product," Mao said. "But I just couldn't resist the new packaging. It matches my uniform."

ferent, they like to make a statement about themselves."[70]

And it wasn't only Moonlight's *consumers* who liked to be different; Moonlight's executives did as well. "This is not RJR as usual," said Kirk Hermann, who, until he cofounded Moonlight, was senior marketing manager for RJR's Salem, Vintage, More and Now brands. "We're a very different group of folks with a very different approach to the market."[71]

Indeed, RJR and Philip Morris both took a markedly different approach to the market—the approach of waging a guerrilla war alongside their conventional war. But make no mistake, even though their conventional troops of Camel and Marlboro were complemented by Jumbos and Dave's, the people and the organizations were very much the same. The smoke screen was added just to make cash registers sing.

CHAPTER 5 # Use Lines of Communication to Your Advantage

The Chairman speaks:

"This new videoconferencing technology stinks! Davis, you look like you're being dubbed in a bad kung fu flick."

MAO

Use Lines of Communication to Your Advantage

> The most important considerations for [the enemy] are that . . . her lines of communication be intact. It is not to her advantage to wage war over a vast area with disrupted lines of communication. She cannot disperse her strength and fight in a number of places, and her greatest fears are . . . disruption of her lines of communication. If she can maintain communications, she will be able at will to concentrate powerful forces speedily at strategic points to engage our organized units in decisive battle.
>
> —Mao Tse-tung

Use Lines of Communication to Your Advantage

Dominant competitors don't necessarily speak clearer than challengers, but they frequently speak louder. The competition can use the mega-megaphone of the mass media to drown out upstarts.

We cannot outscream the competition, but we can break their walkie-talkies. We can disrupt their traditional lines of communication.

We can also build new, alternate lines ourselves.

Their Rules: Whoever shouts the loudest gets heard.

Our Rules: Whoever reaches the most people most intelligently gets heard.

- **Hard Candy** clawed its way into the cosmetics industry—not by screaming, but by whispering in the ears of celebs.

- **Calvin Klein** broke the traditional lines of

IN THE BOARDROOM

communication in the perfume industry, and built new ones that worked to its advantage.

- **Gateway** had limited communications resources at its disposal, and it used all of them to their fullest—right down to the company's boxes.

Communication breakthrough. Communication breakdown. They're both a part of the guerrilla campaign.

Hard Candy: From Dorm Bathroom to Fashion Runway

Dineh Mohajer is living proof that you need not have an MBA to rule in business. You don't even need any money. All you need is a good idea and guerrilla instincts. "I can't comprehend being chairman of a cosmetics empire," says Mohajer. "It freaks me out!"[72]

While she may not sound like your typical CEO, and despite being "freaked out" by it, Mohajer (pronounced "mo-HAH-zhur") *is* a chairman of a cosmetics empire. Her empire, called "Hard Candy," revolutionized both the nail enamel and teen cosmetic industry, generating $12 million annually in worldwide sales.[73]

In truth, Mohajer *was* chairman of a cosmetics empire . . . until she sold Hard Candy to LVMH Moet Hennessy Louis Vuitton for an undisclosed sum ("lots," as she would say) in May of 1999 (though Mohajer remains with the company as creative director).[74]

But Hard Candy's ultimate acquisition by an industry Goliath cannot take anything away from its meteoric, guerrilla rise to success.

The Dirty Little Secret

To trace Hard Candy's beginnings you need to start in the toilet. No kidding. That's where Mohajer, her sister and her boyfriend concocted Hard Candy's "funky shades" as she describes them.[75] Motivated by the "need" for nail polish to match her blue Dolce & Gabbana sandals, Mohajer whipped up a batch for herself, and, prompted by rave reviews at a family wedding, she pushed her new wares at the fashionable Los Angeles department store Fred Segal.[76]

> **To trace Hard Candy's beginnings you need to start in the toilet. No kidding. That's where Dineh Mohajer, her sister and her boyfriend concocted their "funky shades."**

The Fred Segal manager was not too impressed by Mohajer's colors, nor was she impressed by the potential price.

"We were talking about how much we would sell it to [Fred Segal] for, and how much the store would have to sell it for, and then this girl who was, like sixteen came running over and said, 'Oh my God, I love these! I have to buy these. How much are they?'" Mohajer recalls. "We didn't know, but a salesgirl immediately said eighteen dollars a bottle. The girl's mother's eyeballs practically dropped out of her head, but the daughter was having a fit and the mother bought them. Four of them cost, like, seventy-five dollars. The owner turned to me and said, 'Okay, bring me two hundred more tomorrow.' "[77]

And so Mohajer returned to her toilet to whip up some more, in a hurry.

Gritty Product Placement

Hard Candy would have been a blip in the footnotes of cosmetics history had Mohajer not stumbled upon a simple, but elegant guerrilla tactic: "She pushed as many bottles of her product on as many celebrities as possible." She once left a case of Hard Candy in a Mercedes belonging to supermodel Naomi Campbell. A month later, Campbell might just as well have been a walking Hard Candy billboard.[78]

One of Hard Candy's early adopters, Shirley Manson, lead singer of the band Garbage, glows, "They were ahead of everybody with their fabulous colors."[79]

Pamela Anderson, Tori Spelling, Anna Sui and Courtney Love all sported Hard Candy. Even Dennis Rodman slapped it on. Alicia Silverstone hyped it on the David Letterman show.

"I was watching," recalls Mohajer, "and I thought:

Hey, I mixed that in my toilet! Is she sure she wants to be wearing that?"[80]

With free publicity, outrageous colors and outrageous names like "Porno," "Fetish," "Scam" and "Jailbait Vegas," Hard Candy quickly came out of the latrine and into the mass market. It launched a line for men called "Candy Man," which included nail polishes named "Testosterone," "Libido" and "Gigolo." Mohajer hired distributors and developed lip liners and lipsticks, all of which preserved Hard Candy's distinctive packaging: a sleek silver case from which a plastic heart- or star-shaped ring could be removed and worn by wedded consumers to further advertise Hard Candy's grassroots appeal.[81] As the rest of the conventional cosmetics industry scurried to keep up with Hard Candy's trailblazing, Mohajer scoffed at their futility: "Their ads are, like, 'We'll tell you what's hip.' I'm, like, 'Okay, Grandma, tell me about it!' "[82]

Selling Out and Cashing In

Mohajer's decision to sell Hard Candy came as a result of knowing a lot about how to be an insurgent guerrilla and only a little about how to really run a business. She giddily recalls her appearance on CNN's *Business Hour*: "They asked me what my gross revenues were, how much money I've brought in . . . I looked at the camera and said, 'I don't really know' and started cracking up. The guy was ready to strangle me."[83]

"Not really knowing" about business forced Mohajer to cash in. "Basically," she says, "the business just became too much for me to handle."[84] But while she knew very little about how to be an industry Goliath, she had an intricate understanding of what it means to be a guerrilla—and used that understanding to make millions. Not bad for a twenty-two-year-old med school dropout.

It is rumored that Dineh Mohajer and her sister designed a nail polish especially for Mao—"Socialist Sassy"—a royal-blue hue which Mao didn't particularly like. "Red really is my best color," he said.

Calvin Klein Makes a Big Stink in the Perfume Biz

Breaking into the perfume market isn't easy. Inventing an olfactorily appealing product is actually the easy part. It's the process of vying for shelf space with the hegemonic rulers of the industry where things get really difficult.

In 1994, Calvin Klein understood the uphill battle it faced in bringing cK One to the world—or more specifically, to consumers between the ages of eight-

> **Breaking into the perfume industry isn't easy. Inventing an appealing product is actually the easy part. It's the process of vying for shelf space where things get really difficult.**

een and twenty-four interested in a unisex fragrance. But instead of trying to struggle its way into the mainstream perfume distribution channels such as large department stores, Calvin Klein opted to use a different communications *and* sales channel.[85]

Mao was there.

Mao at the cK One print ad shoot. "Whatever happened to quid pro quo!? I thought the deal was that I show you mine, and you show me yours!"

Calvin Klein recognized the fact that not only do eighteen- to twenty-four-year-olds consume perfume, but they also buy music. And so instead of attempting the difficult task of establishing deals with Macy's or Bloomingdale's, they reached out to the then-uncharted territory of Tower Records. Calvin Klein also figured out that many eighteen- to twenty-four-year-olds are university students. And so they reached agreements with Follett College Stores to distribute cK One in college bookstores across the nation.[86]

These alternate channels of communication and distribution brought Calvin Klein and cK One the sweet smell of success.

Gateway: Boxes into Billboards

Computers may be *for* everyone, but they are *of* Silicon Valley and *by* Silicon Valley. Exhibit A: Hewlett Packard. Exhibit B: Apple. Exhibit C: Intel. The list goes on. And it might have kept going if Gateway's founder Ted Waitt hadn't decided to drop out of the University of Iowa and start a computer and technology empire out of his family's farmhouse with a ten-thousand-dollar loan secured by his grandmother.[87]

"I became fascinated by the fact that someone would buy a three-thousand-dollar product over the telephone," Waitt explained. "I hadn't known people could do that with a credit card."[88] They could.

> **Gateway had to embrace its anti–Silicon Valley image to beat Silicon Valley. But how could it really educate consumers about its folksy, South Dakota roots? It was all in the box.**

In no time, Gateway became one the world's top vendors of personal computers—having to experience such growing pains as paving the gravel parking lot in its South Dakota office.[89]

But before the parking lots were paved and the billions made, Waitt and Gateway understood one fundamental key to the company's success: It had to embrace its anti–Silicon Valley image to beat Silicon Valley. But how could Gateway really educate consumers about its folksy, South Dakota roots? It was all in the box.

Every piece of equipment shipped by Gateway—from monitors to mainframes to memory upgrades—came in a cute, black and white cow–spotted box. Why? Because the only places you can find cows in Silicon Valley are in nice nooks such as the Cisco company cafeteria.

Gateway was different from the rest, and the company would use every opportunity at its disposal—even a heretofore plain cardboard box—as a chance to communicate its kinder, simpler roots.

Ask Waitt what's the main advantage of being located in South Dakota: "The biggest advantage is that the weather is nicer than in North Dakota and there are more people here . . . It's not the action capital of the Midwest, but there's no smog or crime either."[90]

Today, with its folksy heritage indelibly etched in the minds of consumers, Gateway has started to modernize its image: with what Waitt has called company "de-prairiefication." "I actually pushed the [design] team to the outer limits of seeing how far we could evolve the brand without abandoning the core elements that made it great," Waitt said. "I even had them explore package designs that didn't include the

Mao was there.

"I had wanted the boxes to look like wombats," said Gateway's Ted Waitt. Mao interjected, "And I said, 'Ted, buddy, everybody loves a COW!'"

cow spots. In the end, I think we settled in a place that really works. It's still Gateway, but with a fresher, more modern attitude."[91] The facelift that Waitt achieved is a combination of high-tech and rustic-country, all proving that you can take the farm out of the company, but you can't take the company out of the farm.

CHAPTER 6 **Force Them**

onto Your

Terrain

The Chairman speaks:

"Mr. Martin, I'm going to have to ask you to take this up directly with office services . . . the photocopier just isn't one of my core competencies."

MAO

Force Them onto Your Terrain

> Guerrilla warfare has qualities and objectives peculiar to itself. It is a weapon that a nation inferior in arms and military equipment may employ against a more powerful aggressor nation. When the invader pierces deep into the heart of the weaker country . . . there is no doubt that conditions of terrain, climate, and society in general offer obstacles to his progress and may be used to advantage by those who oppose him. In guerrilla warfare we turn these advantages to the purpose of resisting and defeating the enemy.
>
> —Mao Tse-tung

Force Them onto Your Terrain

As dominant and expansive as the competition may be, we must do everything possible to ensure that when we engage them, we engage them on our terms—and most importantly—on our *turf*.

When we fight the competition on *their* terrain, we must play by their rules—rules that make victory unlikely for us.

We must use strategy that lures the competition into our territory—a place unfamiliar to them, where we can use all of our guerrilla tools to surprise and wound them.

Their Rules: If the only opportunity to fight is on the competition's home field, we should still try to fight anyway.

Our Rules: If the only opportunity to fight is on the competition's home field, then we should wait until the opportunity arises to fight them on our turf. We should live to fight another day.

IN THE BOARDROOM

- **Target** forced Wal-Mart to play its chic game.

- Two guerrillas—Comrades **Ben and Jerry**—invited industry Goliaths out of their high-rises and into the street.

    The results were tasteful and tasty, respectively.

Target: Tar-zhay Out-marts the Competition

Cheapskate Chic

Kmart tried to out-mart Wal-Mart and lost. Montgomery Ward, Caldor and Woolworth also went the way of the vanquished. Also hurting are Sears and J.C. Penney, which "struggle to eke out even the tiniest growth in sales."[92] So how is it that the Minnesota-based Target not only *survived* the mass merchandisers' melee, but actually *triumphed?* Target's winning streak has come as a result of not fight-

> ## "What Target really did was bring class to the mass."

ing the "mart" game, but instead changing the rules to force others to compete on its terrain. Target's territory wouldn't be in the realm of price or even size—Target would make the previously dull, value-priced retail experience into what some have called "cheapskate chic."[93]

"We had three strategic choices," recalls Gerald Storch, Target's vice-chairman. "To specialize, to become the low-cost producer or to differentiate ourselves."[94] Target unhesitatingly chose differentiation. Burt Flickinger, a retail consultant at Reach Marketing explained, "What Target really did was bring class to the mass."[95]

Target began offering its "guests" (the affectionate term it uses for shoppers) a wide variety of "well-designed, well-made, private-label clothing, which is trendy, very casual and inexpensive," often from well-known designers such as Mossimo. In addition, Target made a strong impact with items for the home—"wall clocks, kitchen utensils, toasters and teakettles"—designed by architect Michael Graves.[96] "We focus on making sure our program is hip and hot and cool," said Target's Storch. "You get clothes that look like they may have come from a high-end boutique, but you paid discount-store prices for them."[97]

Target CEO Bob Ulrich was the mastermind behind the decision to change the rules of engagement by making the competition about quality instead of the quantity (and the prices) that Wal-Mart boasted. "Target was smart to recognize early on that in order to have a distinctive image and to be successful . . . it couldn't just be about having low prices," said Wendy Liebmann, president of WSL Strategic Retail, a New York–based consulting firm.[98] Ulrich himself summarized, "Competitive prices are every bit as important as cutting-edge."[99]

Conscientious Objectors in the Wal-Mart Wars

When asked about others' strategy to tackle industry Goliath Wal-Mart head-on, Target's Gerald Storch called it "absolutely foolish." Storch explained, "It isn't going to work to go against your competitor at their source of strength."[100]

Today, Target's decision to shy away from such "foolish" competition has paid off to the tune of over

Mao with the Target spokesdog, Spot. "Who cares about their prices (or even the products) when you've got a mascot this darn CUTE!"

ion—about equal to the value of Sears, Roe-
Co., Federated Department Stores, J. C. Penney Co., Amazon.com and Nordstrom . . . combined.[101]
Meanwhile, Target has been promoted by such cutting-edge hipsters as Lauren Bacall and Robert Red-
ford. Oprah Winfrey refers to it in mock French, with a
soft *g*—TarZHAY.[102] However it's pronounced, Target
forced the retail game to be played on its own cool
court, and the results have been right on the you-
know-what.

Ben & Jerry's Recipe for Creaming the Doughboy

You might not know it from looking at them, but Ben Cohen and Jerry Greenfield can wage a fairly vicious guerrilla war. A slingshot full of Ben & Jerry's can deliver a pretty punishing blow.

In the mid-1980s, ice cream Goliaths Frusen-Glädjé and Häagen-Dazs learned that the hard way when they tried to freeze Ben & Jerry's out of numerous East Coast distribution channels.

Ben and Jerry understood that to beat industry giants (Frusen-Glädjé was owned by Kraft and Häagen-Dazs by Pillsbury), B&J would have to fight them on their own terrain. "Trying to sue a company the size of Pillsbury would be futile, so we tried to bring

> Ben said, "They tried to fight us in court, but we fought them in the public's mind instead. And that's always been our kind of turf."

them to our turf," Jerry said. "It was kind of fun being the little guy doing guerrilla warfare. I was a one-person picket line in front of the Pillsbury factory in Minneapolis."[103] Ben added, "They tried to fight us in court, but we fought them in the public's mind instead. And that's always been our kind of turf."[104]

Ben & Jerry's took out a classified ad in *Rolling Stone* asking readers to "help two Vermont hippies fight the giant Pillsbury corporation."[105] They gave away thousands of bumper stickers that taunted, "WHAT'S THE DOUGHBOY AFRAID OF?"[106] They unleashed a

Mao, pictured with Comrades Ben and Jerry at the launching of two new flavors: Commie Crunch and Red Star Cherry Delight.

barrage of billboards and airplane banners stating, "HÄAGEN, YOUR DAZS ARE NUMBERED."[107] They even had a radio jingle where a bouncy doo-wop group sang, "There ain't no Häagen, There ain't no Dazs; There ain't no Frusen, There ain't no Glädjé."[108]

All this guerrilla aggression from what the *New York Times* once called "inspirational ice cream."[109]

Fighting on their own terrain has been Ben & Jerry's trademark from the beginning—even when that terrain was their first store, converted out of an old gas station. They've consistently countered the ice cream establishment with outlandish flavors like "Chunky Monkey" and "From Russia with Buzz," all packaged in distinctive, seemingly hand-decorated pints. Of course, the art of making their unconventional ice cream had to come from the most conventional of places: a five-dollar correspondence course from Pennsylvania State which Ben and Jerry passed "with flying colors because of its open-book test."[110]

In the end, Ben & Jerry's built a delicious empire by taking on the enemy on their own turf: whether it was by picketing in style, retailing on a budget, or test-taking . . . with a little bit of sneak-peeking.

CHAPTER 7 **Force Them to Decentralize Power**

The Chairman speaks:

"It just seems like every time we do our management retreat, all we ever do is sit around and discuss what we already know: we've got to go out there and bring in more money!"

Force Them to Decentralize Power

> We must make war everywhere and cause dispersal of [the enemy's] forces and dissipation of his strength. Thus the time will come when a gradual change will become evident . . . and when that day comes, it will be the beginning of our ultimate victory.
> —Mao Tse-tung

Force Them to Decentralize Power

Our bigger, badder competitors are only bigger and badder as long as they are able to reside in one place inside their impenetrable fortress.

We cannot beat the competition by trying to break down the gates of their castles.

We cannot beat the competition by lining up our resources against theirs, attacking and hoping we achieve a miracle.

We beat the competition by forcing them to disperse, inviting them onto our turf, and taking them on individually. Our army against theirs, we lose. Our individual against their individual, we win.

Their Rules: United we stand.

Our Rules: Divide, and we conquer.

- Basketball apparel upstart *AND1* schooled **Nike** in one-on-one.

- **Jägermeister** forced the liquor industry giants to disperse into every bar in America.

Both won. Hands down.

IN THE BOARDROOM

AND1 Slam-dunks Nike on the Blacktop

Basketball footwear and apparel startup AND1 challenged Nike in a game of cutthroat hoops—and they were winning. They were winning not because of *what* they were playing, but *where*. Nike could have beaten AND1 by playing against them in stadiums, on network television and with professional athletes. AND1 recognized this, and took on Nike on its own turf—in the playground, on the blacktop.

But AND1 was also beating Nike by forcing them to play *one-on-one* instead of one-on-thousands. Such is the nature of AND1's guerrilla campaign against Nike that landed the company on *Inc.* magazine's list of the five hundred fastest growing companies in America[111] and catapulted it from a $1 million upstart in 1993 to a $150 million "playa" by 2001.[112]

AND1 Takes Nike to the Hoop

Here's what happened: Nike and the other leading shoe manufacturers have always had to confront the difficulty of dividing their efforts between many different sports—baseball, tennis, soccer and basketball, among others. In the early- to mid-1990s, the leading shoe manufacturers were in the difficult position of relying on celebrity athletes to push their products, while at the same time suffering criticism when those athletes did not live up to society's expectations of them as role models.

This was particularly true in the extremely popular sporting world of basketball. Nike felt the heat when Charles Barkley declared, "I am not a role model. . . .

> **AND1 wasn't going to give a damn about society's expectations. It was not a company of, by or for role models. It was a company of, by and for basketball players. And not just squeaky-clean pros.**

I am paid to wreak havoc on the basketball court. Parents should be role models. Just because I dunk a basketball doesn't mean I should raise your kids."[113] And Converse buckled beneath the weight of social and political pressure by dropping Latrell Sprewell after he tried to strangle his former coach in a fit of rage. Meanwhile, the NBA continued with its saccharine refrain, "I Love This Game."

AND1, a start-up, came on the scene with a mission to hit all of the industry leaders where it hurt them most:

- First, it was going to be *a company devoted exclusively to basketball* (its name references the play in basketball where you get fouled and score anyway—AND1—two points for the basket "and one" for the free throw);

- Secondly, and more importantly, AND1 *wasn't going to give a damn about society's expectations*. It was not a company of, by or for role models. It was a company of, by and for basketball players. And not just squeaky-clean pros. It was a company for the gritty street-ball players who never get paid a dime, but give the game the heritage upon which it stands.

AND1 initially established itself as "the street-level alternative to mighty Nike"[114] through a series of trash-talking T-shirts:

- "YOUR GAME'S AS UGLY AS YOUR GIRL"

- "RESPECT THE GAME, LEAVE THE COURT"

- "I'M SORRY. I THOUGHT YOU COULD PLAY"

- "I DRIVE BY YOU SO MUCH I SHOULD PAY YOU A TOLL"

- "I'M THE BUS DRIVER, I TAKE EVERYBODY TO SCHOOL"

- "CALL 911, I'M ON FIRE"[115]

Underground Communications

AND1 solidified its position as the b-ball company with street-cred through an ingenious and simple communications campaign: It created the "AND1 Mix Tape"—a compilation of video clips of playground legends displaying amazing moves on inner-city basketball courts—all accompanied by a soundtrack of prominent hip-hop acts.

Nike's reel would include NBA highlights of Michael Jordan and Vince Carter. AND1 had a tape of its own stars: "Skip to My Lou," "Headache," "Half Man, Half Amazing," "Future," "Aircraft," "Sik Wit Dit" and "Hot Sauce." These guys never played at Madison Square Garden. Their turf was street-ball meccas like Harlem's Rucker Park. This was AND1's turf. It was their jungle, and if Nike was going to beat them, it would have to beat them there.

Initially, AND1 distributed twenty-five thousand copies of the "Mix Tape" on its turf—playgrounds, parks and clubs. In September 1999, it started distributing the tape through retail establishments such as Foot Action. The mix tape was offered as a party favor with any in-store purchase—irrespective of whether that purchase had been a pair of AND1s or Air Jordans.

In roughly three weeks, Foot Action had distributed two hundred thousand tapes. "The tapes made us real in a way thirty-second commercials could not," said AND1's chairman, who goes by the nickname, "the Franchise." "We had to realize that the playground lifestyle we're trying to market can't be summed up with just a thirty-second spot." Franchise neglects to mention that at that time AND1 could hardly afford to pay for thirty-second spots to two hundred thousand of its targeted consumers. But it could afford to distribute what was effectively an infomercial set to the authentic soundtrack of hip-hop.

The Guerrilla Spokesman

AND1 was just getting started. We return to Converse's decision to drop Latrell Sprewell. After serving out his suspension, the cornrowed forward returned to the NBA with the New York Knicks. "By then," wrote Larry Platt, author of *Keepin' It Real: A Turbulent Season at the Crossroads With the NBA*, "he had supplanted Mike Tyson and Dennis Rodman as sport's preeminent antihero."[116]

Who better to serve as AND1's spokesperson? "We

have to do things other brands aren't willing to do, like signing Sprewell," explained AND1's CEO, who uses the name "Lottery."

Not only did AND1 sign Sprewell, it used him in a thirty-second television commercial that aired more than two hundred times during the 1999 NBA playoffs (by that time, the company had more than sufficient revenues to bankroll such an endeavor). The spot was called "American Dream," and it featured Sprewell sitting in front of a mirror while his hair was being styled into cornrows, with a Jimi Hendrixesque version of "The Star-Spangled Banner" in the background. "I've made mistakes, but I don't let them keep me down," Sprewell muses. "People say I'm what's wrong with sports today. People say I'm America's worst nightmare. I say I'm the American dream."

The decision to use Sprewell came after much deliberation inside AND1. "We spent about twelve hours screaming around a conference room and what we ended up with was a good kick in the ass to get the brand back at the playground level where it belongs," said AND1's Lottery. "We're a grass-roots basketball brand by design and necessity, so that means we have always been guerrilla to some degree. But this was a crossroads where we decided if we were going to be the ballplayers' brand, we'd have to speak to them directly—that means where people are playing for the love of the game, not the NBA."[117]

AND1's Franchise continued, "To a high-school ballplayer, Sprewell *is* the American dream—a self-made, NBA all-star. And if you're comfortable with a different style, a different fashion, then you totally respect what someone like Spree is all about."[118]

If there had ever been any doubt that AND1 was *the* basketball company of, for and by the people, "American Dream" put that to rest. "Other companies aren't keen around the hood," said blacktop star Tim "Headache" Gittens, "AND1 comes through for us."[119] A year later, AND1 came through again with its gritty approach to hoops, this time by using another spokesperson "known for unruly behavior"[120]—just-fired Indiana University basketball coach Bobby Knight.[121] An AND1 spokesperson explained the decision to bring in another b-ball bad-boy: "Bob Knight is a perfect fit."[122]

Nike Attempts Counterinsurgency

By 2001, Nike had seen quite enough of this pesky upstart. It could no longer rely exclusively on its NBA headliners to propel its image. It could no longer appear to be an all-sports-to-all-people company.

> **The great Goliaths of Swoosh created "Freestyle," a 60-second advertisement that was a more polished, better produced version of the AND1 mix tape.**

Nike would have to be a hard-core basketball company. And it would have to mirror much of AND1's gritty street image. In short, Nike would have to launch a counterinsurgency effort against the guerrillas of AND1.

The great Goliaths of Swoosh created the Web site nikebasketball.com and gave the world "Freestyle" a sixty-second advertisement that initially ran in conjunction with Nike's sponsorship of the 2001 NBA All-Star Game. The spot featured mostly unknown players displaying street-ball moves—acrobatic dribbling, no-look passes and eye-popping fakes—all to a rhythmic hip-hop beat consisting of squeaks, dribbles and whistles: the sounds of the game. Nike's ad was a more polished, better produced version of the mix tape.

"We were interested in something that would turn kids on to basketball so they'd pick up the ball and play," said Hal Curtis, a creative director and art director at Nike's advertising agency, Wieden & Kennedy. "We wanted to communicate that basketball is a game about freedom and self-expression and individuality."

Opting for AND1's soft-sell style, Nike chose to include its brand only in passing—the swoosh

Mao in a previously unreleased outtake of Nike's "Freestyle" spot.

appears in the lower corner of the ad during its final seconds. "It doesn't have any shoe shots," said Curtis. "It's more about celebrating the game. It seems to rise above selling a sneaker, though obviously that's what we want to have happen."[123]

Later, to mimic the effect of the mix tape even more closely, Nike released a two-minute-and-thirty-second version of "Freestyle" and aired the faux music video on MTV.

"With 'Freestyle,' we saw that there's a really powerful connection between sport and music," said Trevor Edwards, Nike's U.S. vice president of brand marketing. "That's how we got to MTV and said here's a new way to communicate with consumers other than just a thirty-second advertising piece." Edwards added, "You find new ways [for] people to look at basketball. It's not just about the greatest NBA basketball player; it's also about what people do in their backyards everyday."[124]

Nike's counterinsurgency effort to reconnect with people in their backyards worked. People started buying Nike's sneakers in greater numbers. They flocked to nikebasketball.com to watch "Freestyle" and ogle Nike's products.

Still, it was too late: AND1 had become an immovable force in the industry. The insurgent, while still

Mao was there.

Mao got game. Mad game. Here, "The Chairman," as he's called on the blacktop, displays his trademark crossover dribble move in the AND1 street-ball tournament.

not as powerful as the Nike Goliath, could not be removed from the court. AND1's Lottery dismisses Nike's newfound popularity, "I dare you to find a swoosh on anybody's arm who doesn't work at Nike."[125]

He may be right. But regardless of who ultimately wins this guerrilla game of insurgency and counterinsurgency, AND1 has proven that you can take Goliath to the hole if you play him one-on-one, on your home court.

Incidentally, maybe one of AND1's most ingenious

guerrilla achievements is that it was able to build its street rep while its founders emerged not from the backboards of Harlem, but from the chalkboards of Wharton—School of Business, that is. Nice moves by AND1 chairman Seth "the Franchise" Berger and his boyhood buddy CEO Jay "Lottery" Coen.

Jägermeister: The Sexiest Revolutionary Army Ever Assembled

It has been called "Robitussin dressed as a liqueur and gussied up as a German import."[126] Others describe it as "one part root beer and two parts Vicks Formula 44." They say it "tastes bad and wakes up even worse." And there are those who deem it the "NyQuil Night Train."[127] It is served on tap in bars at a taste- (and mind) numbing "colder than ice" temperature of 4°F.[128]

It is called Jägermeister—meaning the "hunt master" in German. And it has become one of the top-selling liqueurs in the United States—ranking third in sales after Bailey's and Kahlua.[129]

To understand Jägermeister's transformation from digestive-for-the-old to bender-for-the-young, you needn't go any further than Sidney Frank, "the Jägermeister Man." The Sidney Frank Importing Co. has been importing Jägermeister since 1972. It was Frank's decision to initially forego all traditional advertising in favor of event-based promotions that led to Jägermeister's cult status by the 1990s.

Frank recognized that Jägermeister didn't have the resources to battle industry giants in their arena of slick, expensive advertising. And so he created a small band of bold warriors that would infiltrate pubs throughout the land, forcing the competition to disperse.

In 1988, Frank hired his first "Jägerette"—the first of what is now an army of hundreds of young, attrac-

> **Jägermeister didn't have the resources to battle industry giants in their arena of slick, expensive advertising. So it created a small band of bold warriors—the "Jägerettes."**

tive and charismatic women who "stage Jägermeister parties in taverns and bars around the country—sort of a variation on the Tupperware theme."[130]

The Jägerettes (and now, Jägerdudes as well) work the crowd, handing out free hats, T-shirts and samples of "Jäger." Such Jäger promotions cost Frank about $7 million annually—far less than even the most conservative advertising campaign might.[131]

Jägermeister has expanded its nontraditional advertising efforts through its Jägermeister Music

Mao was there.

Mao at his local dive bar getting some affection from the Jägerettes. "To be honest, with those smiles, if either of them encouraged me to drink rubbing alcohol, I'd probably do it."

Tour and a heightened Web presence. A testimonial on the Jägermeister Web site once boasted, "Funny how most Jäger stories contain the term 'black out.'" Frank explains, "It goes down so smooth, that sometimes people drink too much of this."[132]

Indeed, many people have been drinking too much of this stuff. And it is mostly thanks to the Jägerettes and Jägerdudes: modern-day guerrilla warriors bringing libation, liberty and the pursuit of happiness.

CHAPTER 8

The Element of Surprise

The Chairman speaks:

"Good afternoon. This performance evaluation won't take too long. We just have a few questions about some charges on your corporate American Express card."

The Element of Surprise

"Although the element of surprise is not absent in orthodox warfare, there are fewer opportunities to apply it than there are during guerrilla hostilities.

In guerrilla warfare, select the tactic of seeming to come from the east and attacking from the west; avoid the solid, attack the hollow; attack; withdraw; deliver a lightning blow, seek a lightning decision. When guerrillas engage a stronger enemy, they withdraw when he advances; harass him when he stops; strike him when he is weary; pursue him when he withdraws. In guerrilla strategy, the enemy's rear, flanks, and other vulnerable spots are his vital points, and there he must be harassed, attacked, dispersed, exhausted and annihilated."

—Mao Tse-tung

The Element of Surprise

Our competition would like to engage us in a fifteen-round title fight that is announced, promoted and thoroughly planned. While we certainly plan, we are not interested in such a formal "engagement." What we want is to hit our enemy from behind with a few, painful jabs and then run away.

Their Rules: Stand up to your competition, ask them to "put up their dukes," and then "fight them like a man."

Our Rules: There are no "official" rules of engagement. This is war. A fight to the death. The name of the game is winning—destroying the competition—and we must do so by any means necessary.

Maxim magazine and **Virgin** grew from guerrillas into established behemoths through hit-and-run tactics. Now they can simply hit and stay.

IN THE
BOARDROOM

Maxim's Shocking Formula of Beer, Babes and Butts

"Leave the toilet seat up proudly!" declared *Maxim* magazine's opening manifesto. That was April 1997 when *Maxim* was a humble upstart, distributing a mere 175,000 copies per issue. By February of 2001, *Maxim* had an "unheard of" print run of 3.3 million. "By sheer numbers alone," wrote *DNR* reporter Jim Edwards, "*Maxim* is the magazine world's biggest success story."[133]

But while *Maxim*'s rise to magazine superstardom

While *Maxim*'s rise to magazine superstardom may appear to be the result of a simple formula of "beer, babes and butts," it owes its success largely to an ingenious guerrilla strategy of quickness, speed and surprise.

may appear to be the result of a simple formula of "beer, babes and butts,"[134] it actually owes its success largely to an ingenious guerrilla strategy of quickness, speed and surprise.

Neither Pomp nor Porn

Maxim's roots are in England, where the magazine industry had traditionally been divided into two separate and unequal categories: "literary on one side, pure skin on the other." At the same time, "pure skin" publications were rapidly seeing their sales diminish as video and the Internet made porn increasingly more accessible.[135]

Then, in 1994, a magazine named *Loaded* planted a stake in the nebulous, demilitarized zone between lit and porn. *Maxim* followed *Loaded*'s lead with a rag that "found the sweet spot between frat boys and soccer hooligans,"[136] and wasn't afraid "to talk to guys like guys talk to each other," as publisher Lance Ford put it. "Guys know they have their inner swine rooting around in there somewhere," added editor Mark Golin, "and they're dying to let it out."[137]

Maxim unleashed man's inner swine on the United Kingdom and quickly determined it could surprise the U.S. market with an identical formula. When *Maxim* founder Felix Dennis peered across the

Atlantic, he saw a "sleepy American newsstand"[138] where he could be "the first into the desert with a beer truck."[139]

Popular men's magazines in the United States were meanwhile "occupied with picking up National Magazine Awards at clubby luncheons, carrying on a tradition dating back to *Esquire* in the 1960s, and beefing up 'service' columns in response to *Men's Health* and other narrowly focused interlopers like *Cigar Aficionado*." Ford described the competition as "too earnest and serious." So *Maxim* unleashed a surprise attack.[140]

The British Invasion

The men's magazine establishment in America tried its best to impersonate Paul Revere in its forewarning of the British magazine invasion. *Esquire* editor David Granger shrugged, "It's not a bad magazine. It's just limited in its aspirations and ideas of what a man is." *GQ* editor Art Cooper added that *Maxim* had "lots more in common with MTV than with classical magazines . . . we have no intention of changing."[141]

In the face of *Maxim*'s surprise attack, the magazine intelligentsia did nothing. The reading audience, however, very much did something. Despite the sociological trend of political correctness in the United

States, *Maxim* generated immediate traction (and sales) with young men, specifically, twenty-six-year-old men with a median household income of $62,000—as high as or higher than the household incomes of subscribers to competitors such as *GQ* and *Esquire*.[142]

"It is as if Adam Sandler left his career as a cinematic knucklehead and decided to make a magazine . . . by mating the bawdy Fleet Street tabloid tradition to the untethered humor of Monty Python," wrote the *New York Times'* David Carr.[143] "Make no mistake," added *Maxim* essayist Mike Lasswell, "Women are sick and tired of weepy, turtlenecked boys in touch with their feminine sides."[144]

Maxim's first issue included a feature on "Babe Management," a "six-step guide to getting what you want from the woman you love." The feature included a photo of an attractive young blonde with her pajama shirt unbuttoned, along with the caption: "She just made you waffles."[145] Former *Maxim* editor Dave Itzkoff distilled "the magical recipe that . . . dictated exactly which articles were to run every single month" as follows:

- Three (3) babe features comprising pictures of underdressed starlets of varying degrees of celebrity;

- One (1) sex feature dispensing bedroom advice, illustrated with more pictures of models;

- One (1) personal benefit/service feature providing step-by-step guidance for when you find yourself, say, confronted by a terrorist or eager to build a potato cannon from PVC pipe;

- One (1) true crime/"gritty read" feature that is actually thoroughly researched and reported, and often well written;

- And one (1) humor feature comprising even more pictures of women and punch lines that depend on phrases like "man-paste" and "pierc[ed] taco."[146]

Men are eating it up. According to a poll of *Fortune 1000* CEOs, "investment bankers were five times more likely to read *Maxim* magazine cover to cover than *Business Week*."[147] It was named "Magazine of the Year 1999" by *Advertising Age* magazine.[148]

Maxim has even began to use its reputation to expand into other markets, including men's hair products, with edgy dyes like "Bleach Blond," "Sandstorm," "Black Jack" and "Red Rum."[149] And in 2003, Maxim scheduled two television specials to be shown on ESPN and NBC—the first steps toward a new cable channel called Maxim Entertainment Network, or MEN. "The match between *Maxim* and tele-

> **According to a poll of Fortune *1000* CEOs, investment bankers were five times more likely to read *Maxim* magazine cover to cover than *Business Week*.**

vision is very obvious," said Felix Dennis. "You would have to be an idiot not to see it. Do you think with the number of readers that we have among young men that they wouldn't push a button and see what is on a Maxim channel?"[150]

Dumb and Dumber?

The magazine establishment, meanwhile, has continued to dismiss *Maxim*. "It's dumb and dumber," insisted *GQ*'s Cooper.[151] Maybe "bedroom tactics that rock their worlds" isn't the most intellectually stimulating material. Who cares if it's a guide to "nookie symbolism"?[152] So what if people don't actually read it for the articles? *Maxim* magazine combined "dumb and dumber" content with "smart and smarter" strategy and surprise to whip the competition in its self-righteous, politically correct behind.

Mao perusing a back issue of *Maxim*. Of course, The Chairman only reads the mag for the articles.

Virgin Ambushes the World

Richard Branson understands the element of surprise. In fact, he has been surprising people all his life. The surprises started when he dropped out of high school. They continued with his humble, mail-order record retail business in 1970. By the time Branson started Virgin Records in 1973, surprises were in full swing.[153]

Branson has taken us all the way from the Sex Pistols to a veritable Virgin empire—with more than two hundred companies worldwide, employing over twenty-five thousand people and annual revenues upward of $5 billion.[154] Leveraging the muscle he established in the music industry, Branson has expanded Virgin into finance, soft drinks, telecommunications, planes, trains, cars, wines, publishing and even bridal wear.[155]

But the glue that binds all of these seemingly disparate industries is Branson's highly refined understanding of the element of surprise and the importance of acting quickly.

A Fast and Loose Virgin

When Branson entered the soft-drink industry, instead of conducting a typical, expensive, two-year market-research study that a FMCG ("Fast-Moving" Consumer Goods) company like Procter & Gamble might perform, Branson tested Virgin Cola—a cheaper alternative to Coke or Pepsi—in just one major supermarket in England over a mere six months.[156]

When he entered the airline industry, Branson started with a single 747. Virgin Atlantic now has 26

> **Branson has taken us all the way from the Sex Pistols to a veritable Virgin empire — expanding into finance, soft drinks, telecommunications, planes, trains, cars, wines, publishing, and even bridal wear.**

wide-body jets—each offering such "Virgin touches" as massages and manicures. Branson's test-marketing? "I remember I called up [no-frills airline of the '80s] People Express, and I couldn't get through to them. And I thought, well, they must be doing really well or they're really inefficient. If either was true, I figured, there was room for competition."[157]

In 1998, Branson shocked everyone yet again when "Virgin Direct" stormed into the world of investment funds with a simple premise: "Charge far lower commissions than other investment funds." Will Whitehorn, Virgin's corporate affairs director, said, "Everybody laughed at first, because what relevancy did Virgin have in the financial market?" In its first year of operation, Virgin Direct took in $650 million in revenues.[158]

What's Next—Virgin Brothels?

Branson and Virgin have been moving into spaces seemingly overcrowded by the competition with shrewd strategy, lightning agility and unending surprise. "We look at markets where things have been done the same way for a long time," says Branson, "and we ask whether we can do anything differently."[159] The company mission statement continues, "We look for opportunities where we can offer something better, fresher and more valuable, and we seize them. We often move into areas where the customer has traditionally received a poor deal, and where the competition is complacent."[160]

A combination of better, fresher, greater value and no tolerance for complacency has brought us Virgin Atlantic, Virgin Rail, Virgin Megastores, Virgin Cola,

Mao was there.

Mao with Richard Branson enjoying a Virgin Cola. "I like the sodas," Mao said. "But really, I've been a fan of Virgin ever since the Sex Pistols."

Virgin Vodka, Virgin Cinemas, Virgin Cosmetics, Virgin Bride, Virgin Energy (gas and electric) and Virgin Direct—among others. All the while, Branson—when he isn't busy skydiving or floating balloons across the Atlantic—has been unafraid to surprise himself or the rest of the world. "He's a cross between Ted Turner and Evel Knievel," said David Tait, then Virgin's executive vice president.[161] Add Alfred Hitchcock to that list, and you have Richard Branson: the modern master of corporate surprise.

CHAPTER 9 **Speed Kills**

He Who Hesitates

Is Dead

The Chairman speaks:

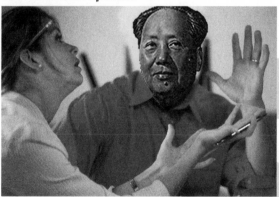

"All I'm saying is that I complained about this to Rothberg in IT three weeks ago, and my stupid e-mail STILL doesn't work right."

MAO

Speed Kills; He Who Hesitates Is Dead

> In [guerrilla hostilities], speed is essential. The movements of guerrilla troops must be secret and of supernatural rapidity; the enemy must be taken unaware, and the action entered speedily. There can be no procrastination in the execution of plans. . . .
>
> [Guerrilla] strategy must be one of lightning war and speedy decision.
>
> —Mao Tse-tung

Speed Kills: He Who Hesitates Is Dead

A leisurely pace is the luxury of the competition. They have the time to ponder and pontificate. They rest on their laurels, reflecting on what they have accomplished and fantasizing over what comes next.

We are hungry and unhesitating.

If we are inactive, we are not winning. We must calculate our next move, and then do it. If there is an element of our strategy that requires extensive, time-consuming planning, we must find a different, speedier way to accomplish our goals.

Their Rules: Take your time, and plan thoroughly.

Our Rules: Take quick action, and plan thoroughly.

Nissan had been snoozing and losing. Now it's wide awake and taking names.

IN THE
BOARDROOM

Nissan's Quick U-turn off the Highway to Hell

To say that Nissan was in a slump in the 1990s would be a bit of an understatement. Nissan trailed its competitors in every key industry category: Honda had made a name for itself with engine technology; Mazda carved out a niche for itself in design; Toyota became known for its durability. And Nissan?

In a 1999 interview, MIT professor Michael Cusumano, who has written several books on the Japanese auto industry, unequivocally stated: "Nissan has never really done anything well." He continued with the accolades, "Their technology is average or below average. Their supplier network is average or below average. They have no distinctive competence."[162]

But what do you really think about them?

The House Was on Fire

Confronting chronically poor reviews and even worse sales, what did Nissan do?

Nothing.

Nothing, that is, until the Brazilian-born Carlos Ghosn was brought in from Renault to give Nissan a complete overhaul. Ghosn (whose name rhymes with "cone") described the complete lack of urgency at Nissan in the face of disaster: "The house was on fire and they were just sitting around."[163]

Ghosn, who earned the nickname, "Le Cost Killer" for his slashing ways at Renault, understood that Nissan itself would be dead in no time if it didn't do something—and do it in a hurry.[164]

> **MIT professor Cusumano unequivocally stated: "Nissan has never really done anything well." He continued with the accolades, "They have no distinctive competence."**

Ghosn acted with lightning speed. Everything—from design to manufacturing to management—was open to review and change, irrespective of how it had been done in Nissan's tradition-rich past. "The situation at Nissan is bad, and some radical change has to be done," Ghosn explained. "There are fundamental management problems. Nissan has to do things that make business sense, not because of habit or tradition. . . . Everybody at least shares this constant: There is no way we can continue to do what we used to in the past."[165]

Change Takes Root

In the face of serious skepticism, Ghosn launched his three-year "Nissan Revival Plan" (NRP) at the end of 1999. The NRP hinged on four principles: "more revenue, less cost, more quality and speed, and a maximized alliance with Renault."[166] Ghosn returned Nissan to profitability from the very first year, having led Nissan from a loss of 790 billion yen ($6.56 bil-

Mao was there.

Mao applauding Carlos Ghosn's revival of Nissan. "I particularly like the Xterra," said Mao. "SUVs are cool."

lion) in fiscal 2000 to a record profit of 183.4 billion yen in fiscal 2002.[167] The turnaround was also fueled by the success of its distinctive SUV, the Xterra (described by one reviewer as "a backpack on wheels").[168] Shiro Nakamura, one of Nissan's lead designers, described the course of Nissan's transformation from leader to follower, "As long as you think you are not leading the world, you copy. We have to change our attitude."

Nissan chairman Yoshikazu Hanawa marveled at the company's rapid about-face. "Ghosn has succeeded way beyond our wildest expectations. The biggest difference is speed. We thought we should change, but we were slow."[169] Ghosn had an intuitive understanding of the fact that speed kills. Nissan could have easily been roadkill by the late nineties; instead, it left the competition in the dust in the new millenium.

CHAPTER 10

An Extended Battle Is to Our Advantage

The Chairman speaks:

"That's right, Rehnmark. But if we just downsize our workforce and bring in some new technology, the whole forecast changes!"

MAO

An Extended Battle Is to Our Advantage

> [Guerrilla units] may be compared to innumerable gnats, which, by biting a giant both in front and in rear, ultimately exhaust him. They make themselves as unendurable as a group of cruel and hateful devils, and as they grow and attain gigantic proportions, they will find that their victim is not only exhausted but practically perishing.

—Mao Tse-tung

An Extended Battle Is to Our Advantage

There is actually no contradiction here: On one hand, we are seeking the lightning-quick skirmish. On the other hand, our goal is a long, protracted war.

To be clear, *our* war—one that is unendurable and exhausting for our competition—is one that is endless, but comprised of countless, quick, biting scuffles.

> *Their Rules: Unless we are winning, we must be losing.*

> *Our Rules: As long as we are still fighting, we are, by default, still winning.*

- **American Girl** hoped that if it stuck around long enough, Barbie would have to invite it over to play. Barbie has had to play—and pay.

- **Fox's** guerrilla strategy was to remain in the game. Its goal was to become thoroughly entrenched in fourth place. It has achieved much, much more.

IN THE BOARDROOM

American Girl: A Decade's Wait and 82 Million Books to Date

From Hooker to American Girl

In 1959, Mattel founder Ruth Handler was inspired by a German prostitute doll that was sold in tobacco shops as a gag gift for men, and promptly produced one of the most popular toys ever—Barbie.[170] More than twenty-five years later, a former schoolteacher named Pleasant Rowland would go Christmas shopping for her nieces and find only Cabbage Patch dolls and the anatomically impossible Barbie. "I was terribly dismayed," recalls Rowland, who said the selection of popular products did not "share the values of my generation of women."[171]

The following year, Rowland took $1 million in savings from the royalties of a textbook company she had started and launched American Girl, a line of history-based dolls and books.[172] By 1998, the American Girls Collection had sold over forty million books and four million dolls, prompting Barbie's mommy—toy giant Mattel—to purchase Rowland's Pleasant Company for $700 million. The sale made Rowland the 294th-richest American, according to the annual *Forbes 400*.[173]

Perhaps the most remarkable part of Pleasant

Rowland's spanking of Barbie is that she did it on her terms and at her own pace. With her unique concept, it was just a matter of time before American Girl dolls caught on to become what Jane Rinzler Buckingham, a youth market consultant, called "the female Pokemon . . . except it's Mom-approved."[174]

Edutaining with Eight Little Dolls

The unique concept behind American Girl is the use of eight multicultural dolls as the focus of historically based stories contained in one of six accompanying books. (Each doll starts at $84, compared to a typical Barbie that sells for $12, while each book sells for $6 per paperback and $13 per hardcover.) The eight different courageous characters from the late 1800s through the mid-1900s include:

- Kaya, a nine-year-old Nez Perce Indian, whose story is set in 1764 in what is present-day Idaho, Washington and Oregon.

- Felicity Merriman, a colonial girl growing up in Williamsburg, Virginia, around 1774.

- Josefina Montoya, a Hispanic girl living on her family's ranch in New Mexico in 1824.

- Kirsten Larson, a pioneer girl on the frontier prairie in 1854.

- Addy Walker, a courageous slave girl who gains her freedom in the midst of the Civil War in 1864.

- Samantha Parkington, an orphan growing up with her wealthy grandmother in 1904.

- Molly McIntire, a girl growing up during World War II.

- Margaret "Kit" Kittredge, a girl growing up during the Depression in the 1930s, and whose family survives by renting out rooms in their house to boarders.[175]

Rowland's use of historical context in combination with the dolls provided its audience ("girls ages seven to twelve—girls who are old enough to read and still love to play with dolls," says Rowland) with both an entertaining and educational experience.[176] "The doll is pretty. It's fun," Rowland explained, "but no doll comes without a book—and that's very intentional, so that the child starts to invest in that doll an understanding of that time period and of that doll's character."[177] That investment, Rowland understood from the start, would require time and patience. But with time, it would pay off.

Mail-order Masterpiece

One element of the larger payoff for American Girl was that it would achieve all of its sales either through the American Girl catalog (it mails over fifty million annually, making it one of the top twenty-five consumer catalogs in the United States), or on-line (its site, www.americangirl.com, includes a "Wish List" that forty-four thousand girls e-mailed to parents or grandparents in its first month of operation).

> **Imagine: over eighty-two million books and seven million dolls to date – all without the help of Toys R Us or even FAO Schwartz.**

Imagine: over eighty-two million books and seven million dolls to date—all without the help of Toys R Us or even FAO Schwartz.[178]

"We did not have the muscle to compete in getting shelf space," Rowland said in 1993. "Our product was subtle. There was a lot of depth that would not be immediately recognizable in a retail environment." Rowland also understood that time was an asset for

American Girl: "We don't want the idea to have such a white-hot flame that it burns itself out." Stephen Schwartz, a toy developer and a former top executive at Hasbro, added, "The big guys spend so much money advertising, when someone can quietly sneak in and build such a business, you have to understand what a beautiful job Pleasant Rowland has done."[179]

Much, Much More than a Doll and a Book

The American Girls Collection has quietly, sneakily and patiently expanded into a massive empire. Today, American Girl dolls are behind only Barbie and Bratz Dolls in sales, but American Girl is far, far more than just a doll and a book. "She's also . . . a video. And a CD-ROM. And a girl's clothing line. And a magazine. And a board game. And an electronic personal organizer. And a backpack. And a [thirty-five thousand-square-foot Chicago][180] retail store. And a tea room. And a newsletter. And a sleeping bag. And a musical play. Oops. Did we forget to mention that a TV special is under discussion? Or that the company has quietly requested a trademark for American Boy?"[181]

Of course, if you have a hankering for extra accessories for your American Girl after purchasing the doll and the books, never fear: you can purchase Kaya's Appaloosa horse ($60), Felicity's tea set ($22), Josefina's weaving loom ($18), Kirsten's snowshoes ($10), Addy's winter sled ($38), Samantha's Christmas music box ($16), Molly's bike ($54), or Kit's Basset Hound ($16).[182]

"It's as if *Nancy Drew* had been accompanied by a

Mao at the American Girl tea room with his favorite doll, Felicity. "I like the American Revolution characters, but how long do we have to wait for a doll from the Cultural Revolution?"

Nancy Drew doll," the *Baltimore Sun*'s Mike Bowler explained, "and a complete wardrobe, an exact replica of Carson Drew's roadster, a miniature Nancy Drew flashlight and a historically accurate miniature grandfather clock as described in *The Secret of the Old Clock*."[183]

Spoon-fed by the Jolly Green Giant

Rowland's insights into the time and patience that American Girl would ultimately require started from a young age—not by playing with Barbie, but by playing with other icons of marketing and advertising. "We saw the Jolly Green Giant and the Marlboro Man around the dining room table," she recalled about growing up as the daughter of Edward M. Thiele—president of the Leo Burnett advertising agency in Chicago. "I learned from my father that the great ideas are executed in fine detail."[184] With impressive attention to detail and the patience to win in the long run, Pleasant Rowland has built a veritable American Girl empire. Too bad for Mattel that on that fateful Christmas in 1984, she didn't just "throw another Barbie on the Visa."[185]

Fox: *Married . . . with Children* Was Just the Beginning of the Battle

CBS. ABC. NBC. Goliaths all. But FBC? With flops like *The Dirty Dozen*, *Family Double Dare*, and *Boys Will Be Boys,* this upstart television network was well on its way to being scrapped just like so many of its failing sitcoms. "For the first six months to a year, we tried to be like the other networks in programming," recalled Garth Ancier, FBC's first programming chief. "Frankly, what we learned is if you try to be like the other networks, then there is no reason for viewers to try you."[186] But FBC hung in there.

Lose the Name

The first step FBC took in becoming less like "the other networks" was ditching its name. The Fox Broadcasting Company would no longer be called FBC. It would just be called "Fox." "[FBC] was us trying to sound like a big network," said Jamie Kellner, Fox's first president. "It was stupid."

Fox was to be the network with a different name and totally different programming choices such as *21 Jump Street* and *The Tracey Ullman Show,* which Ancier describes as "unlike anything you could get on a traditional network."[187]

And tradition didn't know what hit it by the time *Married . . . with Children* arrived. Actually, the Bundy household—the ultimate dysfunctional American family—was not enough to break tradition. Al, Peggy, Kelly and Bud needed some help from their "neighbor," a Detroit housewife named Terry Rakolta.

Any News Is Good News

Rakolta inadvertently brought Fox much needed visibility when she undertook a one-woman crusade against *Married . . . with Children*. Rakolta had watched an episode of *Married* and didn't like what she saw. "I find it very offensive," Rakolta exclaimed.

> **The first step FBC took in becoming less like "the other networks" was ditching its name. The Fox Broadcasting Company would no longer be called FBC. It would just be called "Fox."**

"It exploits women, it stereotypes poor people, it has gratuitous sex in it and very anti-family attitudes."[188]

In the months that followed, Rakolta complained to Fox, and wrote letters to forty-five advertisers, prompting one company to pull its ads and several others to seriously rethink their sponsorship. Almost immediately, Rakolta was on *Nightline, Good Morning America, Entertainment Tonight*, and the front page of the *New York Times*.[189]

"*Nightline* and all these network newscasts would do a piece, and then they would show clips of *Married*," recalls Brad Turell, head of publicity at Fox during the Rakolta incident. "They would talk about the Fox network and then give a history of the network. We were trying to do damage control, trying to save ourselves, but at the same time, they were giving us one hundred million dollar's worth of promotion. By the time the furor died down, the public's consciousness of the Fox network had been raised tremendously."[190]

Kellner added, "Terry Rakolta has no idea how important she was in helping to build the Fox network."[191]

The Rakolta incident solidified Fox's viewing audience, while at the same time crystallizing its troops internally. "We were going to succeed," said Sandy

Mao was there.

A rare photo from the *Married . . . With Children* pilot episode where Mao worked as the stunt double for the young Bud Bundy.

Grushow, then a Fox marketing executive. "We were fighting for a cause. We had a very clear sense of who we were and who we needed to be. We were the epitome of edgy and irreverent among the networks."[192]

Fumbling Toward Success

In the years that followed, Fox continued its trail-blazing and irreverence with *The Simpsons, In Living Color, Beverly Hills, 90210, Melrose Place, The X Files, King of the Hill, American Idol* and *24*. Later, Fox achieved great success with low-cost "reality programming," exemplified by such shows as *America's Most Wanted* and *Cops*.[193]

"We had to fumble around a bit before we found out who we were," says Ancier.[194] Fox fumbled its way from the long-shot "fourth network" in 1986 to an industry leader today.[195] Fox is testament to the fact that for guerrilla organizations, half of the formula for success is simply staying in the game.

CHAPTER 11 **There Is No Such Thing as a Single, Decisive Battle**

The Chairman speaks:

"I'm the king of the world! KING OF THE WORLD!"

MAO

There Is No Such Thing as a Single, Decisive Battle

> The strategy of guerrilla warfare is manifestly unlike that employed in orthodox operations. . . . There is in guerrilla warfare no such thing as a decisive battle.
> —Mao Tse-tung

There Is No Such Thing as a Single, Decisive Battle

If our firepower was larger and our army more robust, we might be able to attack the competition head-on, and inflict a single, lethal blow. Alas, this is not the case (at least not yet).

We must not be hypnotized by the allure of the knockout punch. Death by a thousand paper cuts, while not as glamorous as the knockout, still achieves the same goal: defeating the competition.

Their Rules: Go for the long bomb and the grand slam. Always try for the knockout blow.

Our Rules: There is no long-bomb. There is no grand slam. We will not win by knockout. We will win by split decision or TKO; either way, it is still a victory.

IN THE
BOARDROOM

Their Rules: There is something fundamentally gratifying about a single, lethal blow that ends the war.

Our Rules: We must place great value and merit in the smaller, incremental victories—all the while understanding that they bring us ever closer to beating the competition.

- **Amazon.com** has been consistently—and hastily—placed in the same dot-com dustbin as Kozmo.com, Flooz.com, Pets.com, eToys and Webvan, among others.

- **Vince McMahon's World Wrestling Entertainment** has been written off so many times that it's hard to keep track.

Both are still standing, still fighting, and by most unofficial counts, still winning.

Amazon: Amazon.gone? Nope

Jeff Bezos wanted to call his new trailblazing company something magical: "Cadabra," as in "abracadabra." Bezos phoned his attorney in Seattle to bounce the idea off of him. "Cadaver!" his attorney replied, "Why would you want to call your company that?"[196]

And so, in July 1995, Bezos opted for the simpler name "Amazon," something that could only be confused with the world's second-longest river.[197]

Amazon.com has served many valuable lessons in the new economy. Among the numerous sapient insights it offers is the notion that business is not won or lost in a single, solitary battle. The goal isn't fomenting a lone, decisive conflict and winning it. The goal is fomenting a number of smaller skirmishes and winning them. And when you lose, the goal is living to fight another day.

Always the Scientist

Jeff Bezos has always understood the importance of trial and error. He is, at heart, a scientist. Bezos refined his understanding of experimentation as a youngster. At fourteen, he turned his family's garage into a laboratory, attempting to convert a vacuum cleaner into a hovercraft.[198]

Bezos carried his scientific instincts through school, and graduated from college with a degree in computer-science. He then spent four years analyzing stocks for a hedge fund.

It was in the waning moments of his hedge-fund years that Bezos had an epiphany. In May of 1994, the

> **The Internet was simply something created by the Pentagon to keep its network computers connected in the event of a nuclear attack. It was "a largely commercial-free zone."**

thirty-year-old Bezos started to explore the promise of the Internet.[199]

The Internet was, at that time, simply something created by the Pentagon to keep its network computers connected in the event of a nuclear attack. The Internet was not something to facilitate business. It was "a largely commercial-free zone."[200]

And there was Bezos in front of his computer in his thirty-ninth-floor office in midtown Manhattan, and staring him in the face was a staggering Net usage statistic: The Internet was growing at a rate of 2,300 percent a year. "It was a wake-up call. I started thinking, okay, what kind of business opportunity might there be here?" Bezos recalls, "I'm sitting there thinking we can be a complete first mover in e-commerce."[201]

It is one thing to be first to market. It is quite another to be first to market with something of value. Books, it turned out, were quite valuable. And because they were among "the most highly databased items on the planet," books were quite Net-friendly as well.[202]

No Regrets

With a vision and a mission fueled by what he describes as "regret-minimization," Bezos uprooted himself and started raising money from friends and family. His father Mike recalls, "When he called and said he wanted to sell books on the Internet, we said, 'The Internet? What's that?'"[203] Shortly thereafter, they—and the rest of the world—understood.

Barnes and Noble Strikes Back

It didn't take long for the Goliaths of the book world to understand as well. A year later, barnesandnoble.com came on the scene. George

> Bezos' father recalls,
> "When he called and said
> he wanted to sell books
> on the Internet, we said,
> 'The Internet? What's that?'"

Colony, president of Forrester Research, a prominent technology-analysis firm, awarded a new moniker to the company: "Amazon.toast."[204] But Amazon's sales only expanded in the face of barnesandnoble.com, prompting a new entry into the dot-com lexicon: "getting Amazoned"—which means "to get knocked out by an Internet competitor."[205]

The arrival of barnesandnoble.com wasn't the first time people had given Amazon a death sentence. Bezos jokes, "We've been called Amazon.con, Amazon.bomb, and, my favorite, Amazon.org—which is clearly because we're a not-for-profit company."[206] "It was a lightning-quick trip from Internet poster boy to Internet piñata,"[207] he added. Critics have underscored Amazon's failure to turn a profit, to which

Bezos quips, "Most people don't know this, but actually we were profitable very early on—for about an hour in [December] 1995. Of course, it was a terrible mistake on the part of the management team, which basically consisted of me. We had to go raise more money so we could be unprofitable again."[208]

When not jesting, Bezos addresses the issue of profitability more seriously, "Look at *USA Today*: It took eleven years to become profitable."[209] And there is where Bezos, ever the guerrilla, returns to his revolutionary roots. Critics crave the knockout blow. Wall Street wants Amazon in the black—now. But Bezos understands that Amazon's fate will not be decided in a split second. And he revels in the continuation of the battle.

Mao was there.

"You the man!" said Amazon's Jeff Bezos. "No," replied Mao, "*you* the man."

"This is still day one," Bezos says. "It's still the very beginning. We're not even in our awkward teenage years yet."[210] While Amazon may still be in its adolescence, it has already been through countless tours of duty in the market battlefields; it will likely see many more before it finishes writing the story of its success.

World Wrestling Entertainment Escapes a Headlock to Pin Ted Turner

"Vicious" Vince McMahon versus Ted "the Tormentor" Turner

"I do not like Ted Turner," says World Wrestling Entertainment's Vince McMahon of the media Goliath who started Turner Broadcasting System. "We're competing against someone who has unlimited sources and doesn't have to make money. . . . He's done all kinds of things to crush us, really. His intent was to drive us out of business. . . . It hasn't worked out, I'm happy to say."[211]

McMahon Draws First Blood

Starting in the early 1980s, McMahon has built an entertainment powerhouse in his World Wrestling Entertainment—then, a private fourth-generation family business based in Stamford, Connecticut.[212] With the WWF (now called the WWE after a lengthy suit with the "other" WWF—the World Wildlife Federation),[213] McMahon took wrestling from a fragmented regional circus into a thriving national showcase by the late 1980s. It was around that time that the opportunities for profit—and competition—became undeniable, at which point Ted Turner decided to enter the ring. In 1989, Turner bought out a network of southern wrestling federations and in 1991 formed World Championship Wrestling (WCW) for the TBS network.[214]

Turner Blindsides McMahon

In 1993, Turner launched his most aggressive attack against the WWF while McMahon was trying to rescue his company from a federal investigation alleging sexual harassment and a concurrent scandal

> **Instead of downplaying pro wrestling's phony and scripted reputation, McMahon outwardly embraced it. He coined the term "sports entertainment."**

regarding steroid use in the WWF. While McMahon and the WWF ultimately beat the charges, it wasn't before Turner "offered big money"[215] to sign several WWF superstars, including Hulk Hogan, Ric Flair and Randy Savage. Turner then positioned his *Monday Nitro* directly opposite the WWF *Raw* program. The

WCW shows proceeded to top the WWF's viewership for more than a year and a half.[216]

Virtually taking a page out of one of his own wrestling story lines, McMahon understood that for his WWF, there would be no such thing as a single, decisive battle—inevitably, he would have his fair shot at a rematch against Turner. Indeed, McMahon came back with a vengeance. His first move was to recognize the need to change the entire face of professional wrestling.

McMahon's Stunning Recovery

Instead of downplaying pro wrestling's phony and scripted reputation, McMahon outwardly embraced it. He coined the term "sports entertainment"—"a phrase that deftly acknowledges both the theatrics and the athleticism involved in pro wrestling."[217] "We think we're in the entertainment business," McMahon explained. "Most producers maintain that wrestling is a sport. That's bull crap. We're selling entertainment."[218]

The acknowledgement that the outcomes of matches were predetermined freed wrestling from state regulations.[219] McMahon candidly refers to the WWF's wrestlers as "athletic performers" who he prizes for their "acting ability."[220] In its filing to state regulators, the WWF explained how it "develops soap opera–like story lines employing the same techniques that are used by many successful dramatic television series," including "good-versus-evil or settling-the-score themes."[221]

By embracing the theatrics of pro wrestling instead of avoiding it, McMahon not only sidestepped regulatory pressures, but also won over new fans who had previously been reluctant to admit their enjoyment of this pseudo sport. "There's that old joke: 'What has two teeth and an IQ of forty? The front row of fans at a wrestling match,' " says Bill Hill,

Mao was there.

After his pro wrestling career ended, Mao became a referee. "Get up, you wuss!" Mao shouted as he counted three, "I could take twice that punishment in my day!"

chairman of the Department of Communications at the University of North Carolina at Charlotte. "That's not the case anymore." Hill continued, "[McMahon] did a lot to take away the stigma of saying you're a wrestling fan. Before that, you were perceived as unsophisticated. Now you can enjoy it without having to defend it as being legitimate."[222]

From Nationalism to Populism

McMahon also succeeded in winning fans back from Turner's WCW by giving his "soap opera for guys"[223] more interesting story lines. Since its inception after World War II, professional wrestling's brawls "drew upon ethnic [and national] hostilities to fuel the frenzy of its crowds and give a larger meaning to the confrontations it staged," writes Paul Cantor, professor of English at the University of Virginia.[224] Pro wrestling pitted heroes like the "All-American GI, Sgt. Slaughter" against such villains as the "Russian Bear," the German Baron (also known as "the Beast of Berlin") and the "Iron Sheik," who boasted about his close personal ties to the Ayatollah Khomeini and who later reinvented himself as the Iraqi "Colonel Mustafa" during the Gulf War.[225] The final chapter in the nationalism of pro wrestling came in the form of the post-Cold War villain named "Colonel DeBeers"—

"a white, South African wrestler with an attitude, who spoke in favor of apartheid during interviews." Colonel DeBeers was a flop as a villain,[226] and pro wrestling searched desperately for a new model for its mayhem.

Vince McMahon badly needed a new bad guy, ideally one that couldn't be stolen away by Ted Turner. In a moment of inspiration, "McMahon finally hit upon the most villainous person he could think of—himself."[227] Portraying himself as the heartless boss who

> **Vince McMahon badly needed a new bad guy. He finally hit upon the most villainous person he could think of—himself.**

oppresses his blue-collar employees, McMahon hit a ratings gold mine. The WWF's heroes—or victims—became "the poor, abused working man, symbolized by 'Stone Cold' Steve Austin . . . his perfect working-class opponent—a beer-drinkin', foot-stompin', truck-drivin', hell-raisin' Texas son of a gun, always prepared to tell McMahon: 'You can take this job and shove it.' "[228]

McMahon Dominates with
Less Wrestling, More "Drama"

McMahon's WWF ultimately pinned Turner's WCW with increasing focus on the story lines instead of the wrestling itself. In fact, an Indiana University study conducted in February 1999 of fifty episodes of the WWF's *Raw* revealed that less than thirty-six minutes of each two-hour show is devoted to actual wrestling.[229] The rest is divided among 1,658 instances of grabbing or pointing to one's crotch, 609 instances of wrestlers or others being struck by objects such as garbage cans,[230] 157 instances of an obscene finger gesture, 128 episodes of simulated sexual activity, and 21 references to urination.[231]

The less-than-wholesome content of the WWF hasn't gone unnoticed by critics who point out that 15 percent of the viewing audience—or more than one million viewers—is eleven years old or younger.[232] Sports journalist Bob Costas confronted McMahon by arguing, "There is crotch grabbing—people grabbing their crotch, pointing in that direction and saying 'suck it'—and eleven- and twelve-year-old kids in the audience are emulating that behavior."[233] McMahon barked back, "You've got a situation where you don't watch—we haven't done any crotch grabbing in over a year. We haven't done the 'suck it' chant that you talk about in a year and a half . . . for the record, we even bleep the word 'ass' in the first hour, not in the second hour. . . . Do you know how many people on a global basis enjoy the WWF that aren't elitists like you?"[234]

While McMahon may be losing the moral fight, he has won soundly at the cash register. In 2001, McMahon bought the wilting WCW from AOL Time Warner and made another acquisition, Extreme Championship Wrestling, to form "the Alliance."[235] The WWE brought in revenues of $456 million in 2001.[236]

McMahon Forgets His Guerrilla Upbringing with the XFL

In his body-slamming of Ted Turner, Vince McMahon closely followed the guerrilla principle that there is no single, decisive battle in an ongoing conflict. Still, it should be noted that in recent years, McMahon apparently lost sight of his guerrilla heritage. In the February 2001 ill-fated inauguration of the XFL—the marriage of his pro wrestling soap opera with the grit of professional football—

> **McMahon lost sight of his guerrilla heritage in the ill-fated XFL. The WWF had its roots on cable at odd hours ... the XFL was on NBC during prime time.**

McMahon decided to launch a conventional attack. Unlike the WWF which had its roots on cable at odd hours, the XFL would be carried on NBC and aired during the prime-time slot.

McMahon had conceived the XFL as an opportunity to return football "to the way the game used to be approached by the NFL when football people ran the NFL." McMahon added, "We're not about a bunch of billionaires who are jock-strap-sniffers who simply want to get their name in the paper by outbidding someone else.... That's not what we're about. We're not going to make those cardinal mistakes that other teams and other leagues have made in the past."[237]

McMahon may not have made the same mistakes as the USFL or the World League, but he did commit the cardinal sin of abandoning his guerrilla roots. "We let NBC down," McMahon said in May 2001 of his mistake that cost the WWF and NBC $35 million apiece.[238] "If you're an entrepreneur as I am," McMahon explains, "it's important to be able to, from time to time, take a swing at things. You have to understand the downside before you do and if you are willing to accept the downside . . . then you go ahead."[239] McMahon has been knocked down countless times, but ever the guerrilla, he understands that the fight ain't truly over until the (market) bell rings.

Mao at the press conference announcing the dissolution of the XFL. "Look, Vince, I was the one who told you from the start that this was a lame idea. My point all along was that if you were going to spend all that time and energy getting first-rate cheerleaders, you might as well try to get a few first-rate PLAYERS as well."

CHAPTER 12 **Never Underestimate the Power of the Masses**

The Chairman Speaks:

"Trust me—this display of multiculturalism was in no way premeditated."

MAO

Never Underestimate the Power of the Masses

> A primary feature of guerrilla operations is their dependence upon the people themselves to organize battalions and other units. As a result of this, organization depends largely upon local circumstances. In the case of guerrilla groups . . . they must depend for their sustenance primarily upon what the locality affords.

—Mao Tse-tung

Never Underestimate the Power of the Masses

Everyone loves an underdog. Why? Because there is an aspirational quality to underdogs. Everyone—dishwashers and garbage collectors, billionaires and princes—views themselves as an underdog in some sense.

And so, when we see an underdog competitor trying to topple an established player—attempting to defy all odds and achieve the impossible—we root for them.

We must harness that power.

The ability to have the crowd rooting in our favor is an incalculable asset in our fight. The public is—as they say in basketball—the sixth man.

Their Rules: The masses do not matter. They are merely observers.

Our Rules: The masses are essential. They are key participants in our revolutionary efforts.

IN THE BOARDROOM

Napster and **Harley Davidson** have both ridden the power of the people in their own distinctive ways. One redefined the music industry as we know it. The other rumbled its way into the permanent pantheon of Americana.

Napster's Peer-to-Peer Revolution

The year was 1987. The place, West Germany. The innovation: ISOMPEG Audio Layer-3 technology. It is more commonly known in its abbreviated form, "MP3."[240]

2½ Days to Change the World

The term "MP3" might have remained just as unknown as its more cumbersome, unabbreviated relative had it not been for the work of Shawn Fanning—an eighteen-year-old who combined MP3 technology with the power of the public to make the most earth-shattering paradigmatic shift the music industry had ever seen.

All it took was a laptop, some solitude, and about sixty hours—without sleep—for Fanning to create Napster.[241] "I'm like that."

> **All it took was a laptop, some solitude, and about sixty hours—without sleep—for Shawn Fanning to create Napster.**

Fanning said, "Once I begin focusing on something, I'll just keep going until it's done. I cut off the outside world."[242]

Fanning may have cut himself off from the outside world for those sixty enlightened hours, but what was to follow was anything but isolationist. Fanning saw his program as "a cool way to build community,"[243] and it did so by pioneering P2P, or peer-to-peer, client-based Internet software.[244] In simpler terms, Napster connected millions of music consumers to each other in a radical circumvention of traditional distribution channels. Suddenly, perfect strangers around the world (with their compact discs now compressed into MP3 files), could share their entire music libraries with each other over the Internet—all at no cost to them . . . or to the music industry.

"It's going to kill off the dinosaurs," proclaimed rapper Chuck D, "and force them to rewrite the way they do business."[245]

By the end of 2000, Napster had attracted the unbridled ire of the recording industry. "I don't know if you've followed the court case," Fanning said flippantly in an interview, "but we've been sued by a few record companies."[246]

Notwithstanding the court cases and the ultimate

purchase (and dissolution) of Napster by publishing behemoth Bertelsmann, Shawn Fanning and Napster had reintroduced the world to the power of the people. *Time* magazine explained that Napster had become "synonymous with the promise of the Internet to empower computer users and the possibility that some kiddie-punk programmer will destroy entire industries."[247]

Mao showing his solidarity for Shawn Fanning and Napster. Mao roared, "Screw Matellica!"

Harley Davidson: People Power
Fuels Hell on Wheels

In 1901, two buddies, William S. Harley and Arthur Davidson, fashioned a carburetor out of a tomato can, and started their foray into the motorcycle business. In the half-century that followed, Harley Davidson's thumping V-twin had rumbled its way into steady profits and a solid place in the American psyche.[248]

But by the seventies and early eighties, Harley's future looked dim. "We had just-in-case inventory," recalled former CEO Richard Teerlink. "We had inven-

> **All Harley Davidson had left was its product's appeal to the masses. And so it appealed to the masses for help.**

tory just in case someone anywhere wanted to buy one."[249] Japanese competitors were delivering inexpensive, high-quality alternatives.[250] The company's steady profits had long-since disappeared, and all it had left was its product's historic appeal to the masses.

"We've been blessed with a heritage," said Teer-link. "But we can't simply rely on the mystique."[251] Seeking to rejuvenate its mass appeal, Harley appealed to the masses for help.

In 1983, Harley lobbied heavily in Washington and convinced the US International Trade Commission

Mao was there.

Mao, pictured on one of his seven different Harleys. Before going into politics, Mao spent a year touring with the Hell's Angels of Hunan.

(ITC) that the Japanese were dumping excess inventory in America. The ITC responded with a special five-year tariff on large Japanese motorcycles.[252]

Meanwhile, outside of the Washington Beltway, Harley encouraged the worldwide growth of HOG clubs ("Harley Owner Groups")[253] and nurtured the explosion of RUBBIES (Rich Urban Bikers).[254] The masses responded with fervor. Harley's sales skyrocketed.

And in 1987, Harley did something remarkable. A year before the five-year tariff was to expire, the company appealed to the ITC—not to *extend* the import restraints, but to *end* them.[255]

Vaughn L. Beals Jr., Harley's chairman, explained, "We asked for help, we got it, we don't need it anymore, and in our simple Midwestern minds, it's time to give it back."[256]

Harley made its appeal to the people, and they climbed on board. Willingly.

CHAPTER 13 # Of the People,
By the People,
For the People

The Chairman speaks:

"Ms. McIntosh, I present you with the 'Comrade of the Year' award, which recognizes you as among the top 250 employees at this firm."

MAO

Of the People, By the People, For the People

"Because guerrilla warfare basically derives from the masses and is supported by them, it can neither exist nor flourish if it separates itself from their sympathies and cooperation. There are those who do not comprehend guerrilla action, and who therefore do not understand the distinguishing qualities of a people's guerrilla war, who say: 'Only regular troops can carry on guerrilla operations.' There are others who, because they do not believe in the ultimate success of guerrilla action, mistakenly say: 'Guerrilla warfare is an insignificant and highly specialized type of operation in which there is no place for the masses of the people.' . . . Then there are those who ridicule the masses and undermine resistance by wildly asserting that the people have no understanding of the war of resistance. . . . The moment that this war of resistance dissociates itself from the masses of the people is the precise moment that it dissociates itself from hope of ultimate victory. . . .

—Mao Tse-tung

Of the People, By the People, For the People

Entrenched competitors become vulnerable by becoming too large, too lazy and too out of touch. They frequently forget about what brought them to their position of power: the masses.

When large competitors are in such a position of vulnerability, guerrillas can harness the power of the people to turn the tide against these Goliaths.

The competition can beat us when it is their army against ours. They cannot win when it is their army against us *and the masses.*

Their Rules: Forget what the people say; we know what's best for them.

Our Rules: Utilize the participation of the people to give them what they want.

- The Web-based **eBay** made a multimillion-dollar market by bringing auctions to the masses.

IN THE
BOARDROOM

- Daymond John had such a clear understanding of the importance of the people in guerrilla campaigns that his company—**FUBU**—acknowledged his public troops in its name: For Us By Us.

  For us, by us—so *buy* them. And the public has.

eBay: The People (and Pez) Make the Biggest Flea Market of All Time

A Lucrative Complaint

In 1995, a computer programmer in San Jose named Pierre Omidyar got lucky. His good fortune was to have his girlfriend complain to him . . . again. She renewed her grumbling about her Pez candy dispenser collection—specifically, about not being able to find other collectors to buy and sell to.[257] By September of 1995, Omidyar responded with what amounted to a labor of love: "AuctionWeb," an online flea market—"a glorious bazaar, an easy-to-browse gallery of delightful surprises," including, among many other things, Pez dispensers.[258] Not only did it earn Omidyar his wife, it also brought the rest of us "the world's online marketplace"—eBay.

Seven Years From Zero Users to Fifty Million

After eBay launched on Labor Day 1995, it took a month to get its first user, and just six months to turn a profit. "The business worked much as it does now: A seller describes his item, sets a minimum bid, and chooses how long the auction will last—between three and ten days. Before the auction, eBay charges a listing fee ranging from thirty cents to three dollars and thirty cents, and then takes a cut of the final price."[259] The eBay business model worked well from the get-go, but it wasn't until the arrival of CEO Meg Whitman in 1997 that things really started to take off toward where they are today: eBay is worth more

> **Whitman understood that for eBay to succeed, community had to come before commerce.**

than the combined value of Kmart, Toys R Us, Nordstrom and Saks,[260] and with 49.7 million registered users, it is also the most popular shopping site on the Internet in terms of total time spent on the site per user.[261]

Beyond Toothpaste and Mr. Potato Head

For Whitman, the world of eBay was a far cry from her previous experiences at Procter & Gamble, Disney, Hasbro and FTD flowers.[262] eBay wasn't about the ideal means of marketing toothpaste or children's entertainment or Mr. Potato Head or a "Happy Thoughts" bouquet.[263] Whitman understood that for eBay to succeed, community had to come before commerce. "Some of the best Net successes aren't about developing products," wrote *Forbes'* Elizabeth Corcoran, "but about creating communities where users can tailor the business to meet their needs."[264]

Community-centric Commerce

When Whitman arrived at eBay, the site made no guarantees about the goods being sold, took no responsibility, and settled no disputes. It was a free-for-all, proceed-at-your-own-risk type of environment—a flea market in the truest sense of the term. All that changed when, in response to user message-board postings, eBay created a system for buyers and sellers to rate each other. In what was the first step toward what Whitman would later call the eBay "community," the Feedback Forum was created: "a sort of peer-reviewed credit-reporting system. Buyers and sellers rate each other and comment on how their business together went."[265] Positive feedback opens the door for continued business, and negative ratings ("A total nutcase. . . . Got the old switcho: nice picture, but received piece of junk.") can be the equivalent of being banished from the village.

Whitman's community-centric approach was put to the test in the summer of 1999, when eBay's systems crashed and service shut down several times—

once for twenty-two hours.[266] As might be expected, the community immediately responded by pouring in tens of thousands of messages into eBay headquarters. But most were not to chastise the company, but to show "the cohesiveness of a community." Whitman recalls, "They said, 'Pick yourselves up, don't worry about it, we're still with you.' It makes you realize that we provide a platform, but the real action and vibrancy of this company are driven by its [forty-nine million] users."[267]

Mao was there.

"Listen," Mao told eBay's Meg Whitman apologetically, "I just had no idea that I outbid you for the Pokemon Pez."

The almost rabid community of "eBayers"—as they are often called—recently prompted the *USA Today* to declare, "People go gonzo over eBay."[268] Whitman explained, "eBay comes from the roots of an open, sort of libertarian, point of view. . . . It's a bit of a Vermont thing. Like, let's not get government too involved here."[269] Whitman's laissez faire philosophy has let an online community flourish, carrying the company from Pez to profits in no time at all.

FUBU: For Us, *Buy* Us

When Daymond John was six years old, he already understood the potential power of the masses. As a first-grader he launched his first successful enterprise by leveraging the market power of his fellow classmates: He sold them pencils.[270]

By the time he was twenty-four, John divided his time between his day job as a waiter at Red Lobster and his night job as an upstart designer making tie-top hats out of his mother's house in Queens, New York. "I would get up at eight, go buy fabrics, make some hats until two P.M., call stores or go try and sell them until four or five o'clock, go to work the dinner

> By the time he was twenty-four, FUBU's Daymond John divided his time between his day job as a waiter at Red Lobster and his night job as an upstart designer based in his mother's house in Queens, New York.

Mao was there.

Mao chillin' out with FUBU's Daymond John and rapper LL Cool J.

shift, get home about twelve and make hats until around five in the morning," John reminisces.[271]

But Daymond John and FUBU—an acronym for "For Us By Us"—really skyrocketed when John's boyhood buddy from Queens, rapper LL Cool J, began wearing FUBU garb in music videos and at high-profile events.

"Our strong association with artists . . . like LL Cool J . . . gave us our initial exposure," recalled John as he explained FUBU's success in connecting with the public. "The principals of the company looked like the consumer, so the consumer can identify with us. The acronym for FUBU: 'For Us By Us' drew a lot of people whether old or young to the company."[272]

The masses quickly converted "For Us By Us" into "For Us, Buy Them." FUBU went from being modeled in the streets by legions of loyal consumers to being sold in more than five thousand stores in the United States and around the world.[273]

"There's so much free advertising out there," John said in a May 2000 interview. "We just really have to find a way to tap into that."[274] By harnessing the power of the masses as messengers, FUBU not only tapped into plenty of free advertising, it also established itself as a fashion powerhouse.

PART TWO **Guerrilla Leaders**

The Chairman speaks:

"You mean I've never showed you guys my warthog shadow puppet!?"

CHAPTER 14 **Qualities of a Guerrilla Leader**

The Chairman speaks:

"Yeah *you*, Jutkowitz. Outstanding job on the pork bellies account!"

MAO

Qualities of a Guerrilla Leader

> All [guerrilla efforts] must have leaders who are unyielding in their policies—resolute, loyal, sincere and robust. These men must be well-educated in revolutionary technique, self-confident, able to establish severe discipline and able to cope with counter-propaganda. In short, these leaders must be models for the people.
>
> —Mao Tse-tung

Qualities of a Guerrilla Leader

While guerrilla leaders use cunning strategy to out-
wit and outsmart the *competition*, they must be open
and forthcoming with their *ranks*. Guerrilla leaders
earn the respect and devotion of their following
by offering a solid vision of the future of their organization.

> ***Their Rules:*** *Leaders are coronated.*
> *They earn their position through*
> *patronage and their connection to*
> *the past.*

> ***Our Rules:*** *Leaders are elected. They*
> *earn their position through effort and*
> *their ability to provide a vision for the*
> *future.*

RCN's David McCourt has a loyal following because he has a vision
for the future. Some have
called it quixotic. Others say
he's overreaching and over-
promising.

Consumers say, "Sign
me up."

IN THE
BOARDROOM

RCN's David (McCourt) Slingshots the Goliaths of Cable

Perhaps the most menacing of all Goliath businesses in the United States are telephone and cable. The Telecommunications Act of 1996 sparked much speculation that the telephone and cable television industries would quickly collide—prompting each to use "its existing network to cut into the hitherto monopolistic market of the other."[275]

With just a handful of exceptions, such as SBC Communications and AT&T/Comcast, the magical convergence of these two industries simply hasn't happened.[276]

David McCourt is on a mission to stir up the stagnation.

Stirring Things Up

McCourt, a former construction company owner, has built an integrated phone, cable television and high-speed Internet service called Residential Communications Network or RCN. RCN now has more than one million customers in Boston, New York, Philadelphia, Chicago, San Francisco and Washington, D.C.[277]

"Sooner or later, all tyrannies crumble," reads one

RCN ad. "Those that keep putting their customers on hold tend to crumble sooner."[278]

Therein lies McCourt's guerrilla strategy: Use the strength of the phone and TV giants—namely their giantness—against them.

From a New York office that looks "more like a guerrilla hideout than the headquarters of a telecom firm,"[279] McCourt explains that RCN will beat the

> **The guerrilla strategy of RCN's David McCourt: use the strength of the phone and TV giants—namely their giantness—against them.**

"entrenched suppliers" because cable and telephone executives have spent their whole careers as monopolists.[280] "You need a new mentality to survive," McCourt explains.[281]

Part of McCourt's "new mentality" for RCN is to hit the industry giants where they are weakest: in the realm of customer service—a weakness that has come as a by-product of their "giantness."

Mao was there.

Mao with his family, after having subscribed to RCN. "I just wanted bundled phone, cable and Web services," Mao explained. "Waiting too long for downloads is such a drag!"

"No empire lasts forever," says another RCN ad. "Especially one that keeps you waiting five hours for a repairman." When RCN customers order a second phone line, they receive a call from RCN's installers—wherever the customer may be—a half hour before they are needed at home for the installation. In New York City, the best Verizon customers can hope for is a four-hour window.[282]

The Crowded Pole

How did McCourt squeeze his way onto "that crowded telephone pole?"[283] Federal statutes would probably support RCN if it took phone and cable providers to court over access. But the courts are the terrain of the giants.

So RCN went the guerrilla route and teamed up with the next rung on the utility pole: electric companies. RCN strings its fiber-optic cable alongside electric power lines and in underground electric conduits—giving them access into the homes of the masses.[284]

Telephone and cable outfits have cried foul to utility regulators about the arrangement. McCourt's response: "They're all whiners."[285] "Monopoly Behavior 101," he says dismissively.[286]

While his war against the industry giants may seem quixotic, McCourt is rapidly turning his crusade into reality. "I've learned not to take wild claims seriously," wrote *Forbes* reporter Daniel Roth, "but this is one David who may well kick Goliath's butt."[287]

CHAPTER 15

Guerrilla Leaders Are By, For, and Perhaps Most Importantly, *Of* Their Troops

The Chairman speaks:

"We're too clever. And too sexy."

MAO

Guerrilla Leaders Are By, For, and Perhaps Most Importantly, *Of* Their Troops

> In a revolutionary army, all individuals enjoy political liberty. . . . Further, in such an army, the mode of living of the officers and the soldiers must not differ too much, and this is particularly true in the case of guerrilla troops. Officers should live under the same conditions as their men, for that is the only way in which they can gain from their men the admiration and confidence so vital in war.
>
> —Mao Tse-tung

Guerrilla Leaders Are By, For, and Perhaps Most Importantly, *Of* Their Troops

To be defined as leader, you need a following.

A following must be earned.

To earn a following, you must earn people's respect.

To earn people's respect, they must see you as one of them.

To be one of the people, you must exist *with* them—not above or below them.

> ***Their Rules:*** *Leaders are* above *their troops.*

> ***Our Rules:*** *Leaders are one* with *their troops.*

- **Andrea Jung** led her army of **Avon** Ladies on a veritable cosmetics crusade.

- **Herb Kelleher** took his company, **Southwest Airlines**, to cloud nine and beyond, all the while with his feet firmly planted on the ground.

Both treated their troops like equals. Their troops were happy to return the favor.

IN THE BOARDROOM

Andrea Jung Leads the Avon Ladies by Becoming One

Reviving a Relic

In 1999, Avon, the beauty products giant, was struggling. During one of the greatest economic peaks in history, the company's profits were sinking to new lows. For most women, Avon conjured a "stale image"[288]—"bubble bath and tacky lipstick"[289]—along with the "Ding-dong, Avon calling" jingle that dates back to the early 1950s.[290] Unless someone did something fast, Avon itself would become history.

Andrea Jung Gives Avon a Makeover

Enter Andrea Jung, the first woman to lead Avon in its 116 years of business. Jung quickly took Avon from "a declining brand that would struggle to survive in the twenty-first century" to one of *Business Week's* one hundred leading global brands.[291] She did it not by abandoning the Avon Lady, but by becoming one herself.

"I wanted to go through the selling experience," recalls Jung. "I was going door-to-door in my neighborhood." By ringing Manhattan doorbells, Jung gained powerful insights about the benefits—and drawbacks—of Avon's products. "She heard customer gripes over discontinued colors, mishandled orders, confusing promotions. One customer chewed her out for showing up with a catalog that didn't offer her favorite skin cream."[292]

Andrea Jung succeeded in turning around Avon not just by becoming one of the foot soldiers in

> **Andrea Jung took Avon to a leading global brand not by abandoning the Avon Lady, but by becoming one herself.**

Avon's army, but also by directly engaging her core customers. Jung introduced Avon's corporate tagline, "The company for women," and created the "Let's talk" ad campaign.[293]

Jung talked . . . and listened.

Out of the Streets and into the Stores

In response to customer feedback, Jung over-hauled Avon. Perhaps the most revolutionary change she instituted was to take Avon out of the catalogs and into the department stores. Historically, Avon's business revolved around Avon reps who receive cat-

Mao was there.

Mao and Andrea Jung finishing Avon's annual charity walkathon. "Compared to the Long March, this was a cakewalk."

alogues, take orders from family and friends, keep a percentage of all sales made and send the orders through to the company that then fills them.[294] Jung, while maintaining the rep model, also started selling a new line of Avon products in retail stores such as J. C. Penney—something it had never done in its long history. It "has a high probability of disappointment," a Paine Webber analyst report predicted at the time. "Nobody thought we could do it," said Jung. "And that just made us want to prove them wrong."[295]

Prove them wrong, she has. By becoming the lead foot soldier in her cosmetics crusade, Jung has restored Avon to the world's leading direct seller of beauty products, with about $6 billion in annual revenues.[296]

Lipstick Leadership

"I think there is a big and significant difference between being a leader and being a manager; leaders lead from the heart," says Jung. "Flexibility is one of the key ingredients to being successful. If you feel like it's difficult to change, you will probably have a harder time succeeding."[297] As for the significance of being the right gender for the job: "I guess it helps," Jung wryly explains. "You know, you go home and you try on a new mascara, and I guess a male CEO can't do that."[298]

Southwest Airlines' Herb Kelleher: Executive by Day, Baggage Handler by Night

Southwest Airlines' Herb Kelleher is one of the most successful executives in the history of aviation. Until he handed the CEO keys over to Colleen Barrett in 2001, Kelleher made a living out of being at one with his troops. They didn't simply *like* working for him. They *loved* it.

Southwest started out in 1966 when Kelleher and his friend Rollin King drew a triangle on a cocktail napkin—a triangle connecting Dallas, Houston and San Antonio.[299] By 1972, Southwest had transferred all of its Houston service from Houston Intercontinental to Houston's Hobby Airport, answering Kelleher's rhetorical question, "After all, why should our customers have to drive forty-five minutes to take a forty-minute flight?"[300]

An Outrageous Company

Since its inception, Southwest has not deviated from its original mission of "short-haul, high-frequency, low-fare, point-to-point service," as Kelleher puts it.[301] And it has consistently delivered on its promise of "positively outrageous service."[302]

"Positively outrageous service" has come as a result of the family atmosphere Kelleher built with his employees. Kelleher gave his explanation of the Southwest family in a 1994 interview: "I feel you have to be with your employees through all their difficulties, that you have to be interested in them personally. They may be disappointed in their country. Even their family might not be working out the way they wish it would. But I want them to know that Southwest will always be there for them."[303]

Bagging on Black Wednesday

For his part, Kelleher himself was always there for his employees. He frequently spent Thanksgiving—the year's busiest travel day—with baggage handlers on the ramp at Dallas' Love Field. Ramp agent Jack Blue Jr. recalls, "On Black Wednesday, the man is out here throwing bags alongside us. He doesn't have to come out here."[304]

For Kelleher, rubbing elbows with employees was neither a gesture nor a stunt. It was his way of staying engaged with his staff and ensuring that the company continued to operate smoothly. "He'll go out with a couple of mechanics and have a few drinks until five A.M., listen to what needs to be changed and go out the next day and fix it," said Steve Lewins, a

> **Kelleher once told a visitor who had recently kicked the smoking habit that it "reflects unfavorably on your character. Do you like being called a quitter?"**

transportation analyst with Gruntal & Co., who has followed Southwest since the 1970s.[305]

Of course, one must question the meaning of "a few" drinks with Kelleher: At the ripe age of 73, he has an "avowed passion for bourbon (Wild Turkey) and cigarettes (five packs a day)."[306] He once told a visitor who had recently kicked the smoking habit that it "reflects unfavorably on your character. Do you like being called a quitter?"[307]

Kelleher's easygoing demeanor is largely responsible for Southwest's family feel. He instituted only three rules for the company:

- Rule No. 1: Under no circumstances shall you leave a company document with the CEO.
  ("I'll lose it," Kelleher laughs.)

- Rule No. 2: Every day is casual Friday.

- Rule No. 3: Don't get your shorts tied in a knot over the rules.

"Now it's a trend in America for businesses to become less stuffy. But people used to look at me like I had a brain tumor of considerable size."[308]

Superhero with Spackle

All told, Kelleher's nearly four decades on the job rendered him something of a superhero among employees. Kelleher dismisses his rock-star appeal: "Frankly, I've never felt like Barbra Streisand. Southwest Airlines is built on low cost, whether or not my

Mao applauding Herb Kelleher's decision to finally step down as CEO of Southwest Airlines after thirty years at the helm. "Herb, we're getting too old for this crap," Mao said. "It takes us twice as long to look half as good."

ugly puss appears. I'm getting to a stage where they have to use Spackle on me, not makeup. If we keep providing the lowest fares, people are going to keep flying no matter the CEO."[309]

When CEO Herb Kelleher finally stepped down in the spring of 2001, he appointed as president and COO the "plain-spoken, chain-smokin'" Colleen Barret to maintain Southwest's family culture. Southwest has continued to "soar while other carriers lost money."[310] In the meantime, Kelleher drives off into the sunset in his fire-engine-red Jaguar—the one with the bumper sticker that implores: "FLY SOUTHWEST. I NEED THE MONEY."[311]

CHAPTER 16 **Centralized**

Leadership

The Chairman speaks:

"Mr. Persons, how many times do I have to ask: Please, please use *coasters* on the conference table."

MAO

Centralized Leadership

> What is the organization for guerrilla warfare? Though all guerrilla bands that spring from the masses of the people suffer from lack of organization at the time of their formation, they all have in common a basic quality that makes organization possible. All guerrilla units must have political and military leadership.
>
> ... Both organization and discipline of guerrilla troops must be at a high level so that they can carry out the political activities that are the life of both the guerrilla armies and of revolutionary warfare.
>
> —Mao Tse-tung

Centralized Leadership

Guerrilla warfare is often confused with a free-for-all. The competition *perceives* our operations as random, disjointed and dispersed, but they are wrong.

We are scattered in our numbers, but not in our vision. The seed of our strategy is cultivated centrally and then scattered wildly.

> *Their Rules:* Guerrillas are scatter-brains, without any real leadership.

> *Our Rules:* Guerrillas have focused leadership designed to leave our opponents scattered and tattered.

- **Oprah Winfrey**'s daytime television show may seem like an open-invitation slumber party, but behind it is a mother who's not afraid to lay down the law.

- **Howard Schultz** had a vision, and subsequently scattered his beans— through **Starbucks**— almost everywhere.

For both, the cup is still much more than half full.

IN THE BOARDROOM

Oprah Wears the Pants in Her Empire

Oprah Winfrey happily admits she cannot read a balance sheet or an income statement. She has no corporate role models. She has welcomed Hollywood stars like Tom Cruise on her show with open arms, but she has declined invitations from AT&T, Ralph Lauren and Intel to sit on their corporate boards. "I just say, 'Guys, I don't know what I'd be doing on your board,' " Oprah explains. "I don't think of myself as a businesswoman."[312]

Soft on the Tube, Firm in the Boardroom

Since she began her entertainment career at a small television station in Baltimore in the 1970s, Oprah has gradually created her own media empire, Harpo (Oprah spelled backwards), and amassed a $1 billion fortune.[313] Not bad for a nonbusinesswoman. But while Oprah's on-screen persona may involve sharing many elements of her personal life with the world—including endless battles against weight gain, and her triumphs over adversity and abuse[314]—Oprah is quite different in the boardroom; Oprah's path to guerrilla success has relied heavily on her centralized leadership. "A shrewd businesswoman," explained a recent *Newsweek* article, "she still signs all the checks of more than one thousand dollars for her Harpo Entertainment Group, and she meticulously scrutinizes the smaller ones that others sign for her."[315]

The quirky combination of centralized leadership and "girls yakking honestly" has propelled Oprah

> **"A shrewd businesswoman,"** explained a recent ***Newsweek*** article about Oprah, **"she still signs all the checks of more than one thousand dollars . . ."**

and her *Oprah Winfrey Show* to the number-one spot in U.S. daytime talk shows for the past seventeen years, despite challenges from at least fifty insurgents.[316] Oprah currently has twenty-two million U.S. viewers, and airs in 107 countries around the world—bringing in over $300 million in 2001 to the Harpo Entertainment Group (of which Oprah owns a bit more than 90 percent).[317]

A Strong Seat at the Table of Contents

In April 2000, Oprah decided to extend the reach of her centralized leadership beyond the television screen and into the magazine world. After having been approached by a slew of publishers, Oprah finally received a pitch she couldn't refuse from Hearst Magazines. *Good Housekeeping* editor Ellen Levine and Hearst president Cathleen Black showed Oprah a complete prototype with a sample table of contents and a book of page layouts. They even gave it a name: *Oprah's Spirit*. With the exception of one minor detail, Oprah hated it all.[318] Of course, that minor detail was their offer to let her have complete editorial control over the magazine.

Oprah quickly went into action by giving the publication a new name—*O*—and overhauling the layout. She began by moving the table of contents to page 2, away from its usual residence in women's magazines—around page 22—where readers have to wade through a slew of ads before they get to it. "At first people said, 'You can't put the table of contents there,'" recalls Oprah. "After a while they just said, 'Okay, Oprah, where would you like it?'"[319]

When she received the news that Hearst was planning to release the first issue paired with *Cosmopolitan* on special display stands, Oprah called the publishers and protested, "I am not going to be used to sell one of your other magazines."[320] Oprah rarely has people say no to her, and her magazine's launch was no exception: *O* appeared solo. "What has been an advantage—even though some people might not

Mao and Oprah off to pick up the latest issue of *O* magazine. "I love the articles," said Mao. "But couldn't they just leave out all those smelly perfume ads!?"

consider it an advantage," says Oprah, "is the fact that I had no magazine experience. Zip. Zilch. None. Zero. And so I came in with an open mind about what could and could not be done."[321]

While Oprah's magazine experience might have been limited, her experiences as a seasoned leader were enough to propel *O* to stratospheric heights in the magazine world. Hearst's Black described *O* as "significantly profitable"—highly unusual, given that most successful magazines usually take at least five years to turn a profit. In 2001, *O* brought in more than $140 million in revenues and currently has a paid circulation of 2.5 million[322]—more than top-sellers such as *Vogue, In Style, Vanity Fair* or *Martha Stewart Living.*

Some have characterized Oprah's winning formula as a combination of "Down-to-earth diva," "control freak" and "silly best girlfriend."[323] Oprah herself says it's more about bold leadership and "leaps of faith." Grinning, she says, "If I called a strategic-planning meeting, there would be dead silence, and then people would fall out of their chairs laughing."[324]

Starbucks' Howard Schultz:
He Decreed Small is "Tall" and
Leads from the Top Down

Howard Schultz had a vision to be in third place. To get there, he had to go on a serious odyssey. Schultz had worked as a salesman for Xerox, and eventually became vice president of U.S. operations for a Swedish housewares manufacturer, when he noticed that a small Seattle retailer was ordering a large number of his company's drip coffeemakers. In 1981, Schultz headed to Seattle to see where all those coffeemakers were going.[325]

What Schultz found was Starbucks Coffee, Tea and Spice—a company founded in 1971 by three entrepreneurs in their twenties who started selling whole-bean coffee at Seattle's Pike Place Market. They named the store Starbucks after the first mate in Moby Dick.[326] Schultz was "so impressed with the then-ten-year-old company's dedication to providing customers with quality imported coffee beans, he signed on as director of Starbucks' retail operations and marketing the following year."[327]

By 1982, Starbucks had built a solid retail business in Seattle: five stores, a small roasting facility and a wholesale business selling coffee to local restaurants.[328]

The Piazza Epiphany

In 1983, as Schultz wandered through the piazzas of Milan, he had a vision that would ultimately percolate Starbucks into the hot spot of the caffeine craze. Schultz was attending a housewares convention in Italy and started to closely observe the social dynamics of the coffee bar. He "became fascinated with the camaraderie between customers and the barista, or coffee maker."[329]

"I saw the relationship Italian culture has with coffee and the romance of the beverage," Schultz says. "The Italian starts his day at the coffee bar and sees his friends there later on. It struck me that this was also possible in America. It had never been done—and we could do it because the quality of Starbucks coffee is unsurpassed."[330] From that point on, Schultz was on a mission to bring the Italian coffee bar experience to America.

Perseverance au Lait

Schultz's vision was not met with a warm reception in the United States. Schultz pounded the pavement to raise venture capital. "I was turned down by

217 of the 242 investors I initially talked to," he recalls. "You have to have a tremendous belief in what you're doing and just persevere."[331]

Persevere he did. Schultz was driven not only by his vision of the Italian coffee culture, but also by a vision of people's need for an intermediate place

> **Starbucks is so damn ubiquitous that comedian Janeane Garofalo says that they just opened in her living room.**

between home and work: a nonalcoholic pub. It was a vision he had for the people, despite the fact that they did not necessarily have it for themselves.

This is where Schultz's aspiration to be in third place comes in.

"Customers don't always know what they want," explains Schultz. "Once they tasted our [coffee] and experienced what we call 'the third place'—a gathering place between home and work where they were treated with respect—they found we were filling a need they didn't know they had."[332]

"This 'third place,'" Schultz continues, "is something that people are so hungry for. We're all so busy with cell phones and e-mails and faxes that the thought of sitting over a cup of coffee in an environment you like comes to life, and that's the Starbucks brand."[333]

Mao and Starbucks' Howard Schultz toasting each other with a cup of joe. "Howard, this is decaf, right?" asked Mao. "You know how jittery I can get with that jet fuel you drink."

Strange Brew Here, There and Everywhere

Starbucks is so damn ubiquitous that comedian Janeane Garofalo says that they just opened one in her living room.[334] And they're just getting started. "These are very early days for the growth of our company," says Schultz. "Our aim is to see more people drinking coffee than eating hamburgers. McDonald's has twenty-five thousand [now thirty thousand] outlets around the world. Well, I don't like to draw comparisons between ourselves and McDonald's, but we are going to get there too."[335]

With a "mere" six thousand outlets under its belt, Starbucks is only a fraction of the way to equaling McDonald's reach, but it has come a long way from its days as a humble four-store retailer. Howard Schultz, through perseverance and a clear vision, discovered that sometimes the best way to first place is through "third place."

CHAPTER 17

Guerrilla ≠

Anarchy

The Chairman speaks:

Mao at his annual "Managing Effectively" seminar. "At this firm, we've made great strides toward breaking the strict hierarchical structures of the past," he said.

MAO

Guerrilla ≠ Anarchy

" Unorganized guerrilla warfare cannot contribute to victory, and those who attack the movement as a combination of banditry and anarchism do not understand the nature of guerrilla action.

A revolutionary army must have discipline that is established on a limited democratic basis. In all armies, obedience by the subordinates to their superiors must be exacted. "

—Mao Tse-tung

Guerrilla ≠ Anarchy

Guerrilla campaigns are only successful when the individuals within the army understand their respective roles and responsibilities.

Although it may be a nontraditional team, it is nevertheless a team. The moment guerrilla organizations take on the disorder and mayhem of anarchy, they will fail. They must have structure and stability to undermine the structure and stability of the competition.

- **Intel's Andy Grove** has taken anti-anarchy to near-autocratic levels. His guerrilla troops know where they stand, because he's quite clear about the way things will be—if and when they step out of line.

- **Diesel Jeans' Renzo Rosso** has created chaos couture, but behind it all is a bell-bottomed master plan.

IN THE BOARDROOM

Their Rules: *Guerrillas are just anarchists—a motley crew of rebel-rousers.*

Our Rules: *Guerrillas are a highly organized unit of rebels inflicting disorder on their opponents.*

Intel's Andy Grove: Ruling with an Iron Fist and a (Micro) Chip on His Shoulder

The semiconductor business is a bitch. Unisem died of obsolescence. Advanced Memory Systems was murdered by management. And Mostek fell prey to a Japanese RAM invasion.

So how has Intel prevailed? How did it weather the storm of chip recessions, a Federal Trade Commission probe and "a nasty public flogging over its flawed Pentium chips in 1994"?[336]

Two words: Andy Grove.

Grove has shepherded Intel through decades of turbulence—not by consensus or democracy, but by good old-fashioned discipline and centralized control.

> Grove has shepherded Intel through decades of turbulence — not by consensus or democracy, but by good old fashioned discipline and centralized control.

No Room for Error

Although Andy Grove encourages what he calls "constructive confrontation," Grove is by no means a portrait of egalitarianism: "The culture, the centralized power, the tremendous profitability—it's a blinding light," said venture capitalist Jack C. Carsten, former Intel senior vice president.[337]

Mao was there.

Intel's Andy Grove comforting Mao shortly before Grove fired him. "There's only room in this company for one Chairman," Grove insisted.

Venture capitalist John Doerr, who worked for the firm for six years in the 1970s, added, "When I was at Intel, one of the most important values was discipline. Andy Grove had no tolerance for people who were late or meetings that ran on without a purpose. It wasn't that he was a hard-ass; it's just the nature of their business. There's no room for error."[338]

Way back in 1971, Grove began his "no room for error" policy by instituting a late list to take note of employees arriving after 8 A.M.[339] In 1984, *Fortune* magazine recognized Grove for his "conviction," shall we say, by naming him "one of America's toughest bosses."[340]

Notwithstanding his reputation for being a tough cookie, Grove has achieved tremendous success with a business model designed around his mantra, "Only the paranoid survive."

The Tough Road to Success

It was Grove who beat out Motorola for the contract to supply microprocessors for IBM's groundbreaking PC in 1979. It was Grove who pulled the plug on Intel's memory-chip business in 1985, forcing the company to focus on more lucrative microprocessors. And in 1994 it was Grove who decided to swallow his pride and offer to replace millions of slightly flawed

Pentium processors—at a cost of nearly half a billion dollars—in an attempt to preserve Intel's gold-standard reputation.[341]

Grove has succeeded by making tough decisions and ruling with an iron fist. And for those who disagree? When critics continued to badger Grove over errors in its Pentium chip, he responded, "If you know where a meteor will land, you can go there and get hit."[342] Not necessarily nice, but definitely effective.

Diesel Jeans and Renzo Rosso's Regimentation of Chaos

Cashing In on Counter-convention and Chaos

"Cut the bullshit. Enjoy life. Laugh," urges one advertisement for Diesel Jeans.[343] Another sarcastically boasts, "All Diesel jeans have been tested on animals."[344] Diesel Jeans and its founder Renzo Rosso have spent the last quarter-century promoting an unstructured, carefree and almost anarchistic image. And they have cashed in by constructing a world of order behind the façade of chaos.

Rosso intentionally removed Diesel from the traditional fashion centers to insulate it from convention. With its headquarters based in Molvena, in the northeastern part of Italy, Rosso implored his designers to "ignore current movements."[345] "Diesel design does not follow established trends," explains its company manifesto. "It is largely unaffected by fads occurring within the fashion circles; it is innovative and at times a bit radical . . . Diesel collections effectively precede trends and do not respond to them."[346]

Diesel's rejection of convention has catapulted it from a stonewashed afterthought to Levi's, Lee and Calvin Klein to a $330 million denim powerhouse employing over one thousand three hundred people worldwide. "Diesel is not my company," says Rosso, "it's my life."[347]

Designing Disorder

One remarkable element behind Diesel's success is its celebration of what many would describe as downright disorder. Its designers are mandated by Rosso to take all-expenses-paid "research trips" every six months under the auspices of "just to be inspired."[348] "Think of a place," wrote journalist Melanie Rickey, "and they have probably been there, photographed it, bought local records, been to jumble sales and just hung out."[349] Tempting as it might be to dismiss such globe-trotting as frivolous use of the company expense account, this is all a part of Diesel's order of disorder. Indeed, when Rosso's designers return to Molvena, their "research" is thoroughly catalogued, synthesized and subsequently reincarnated in the next collection.[350]

Cultivating Consumer Confusion

Diesel's greatest achievement in structured chaos can be found in its individual retail stores themselves. In fact, many stores introduce customers to its mayhem before they can even step foot inside. At the Diesel shop in London's Covent Garden, shoppers are first greeted by bouncers who invoke a "One in, one out" door policy, trying—often in vain—to impose crowd-control tactics on eager shoppers.[351] And once customers have earned the good fortune of actually getting inside, they are rewarded by what Niall Maher, Diesel's director of retail operations, described

> Some might argue that Diesel has made a business out of chaos. What is fundamental to Diesel's success is that it actually controls the chaos.

as an intentionally confusing, overwhelming and disorderly environment. "We're conscious of the fact that, outwardly, we have an intimidating environment," said Maher. "We didn't design our stores to be user-friendly."[352]

Some might argue that Diesel has made a business out of chaos. But what is fundamental to Diesel's success is that it actually controls the chaos. "They realized the best way to get people to buy stuff is not to facilitate their shopping but to disorient

Mao was there.

Mao, thoroughly confused at the Diesel "Denim Bar," whispered to the salesman, "I just think I prefer the Kulters. The bell-bottomed Ravixes make me look fat."

them," said Douglas Rushkoff, a media critic who has written about Diesel advertising campaigns. "Diesel shoppers say, 'I'm not hip enough to get this,' and then in comes the hip salesperson. What makes them hip is that they know how to navigate the space." Maher agreed, adding, " . . . because we want you to interact with our people. You can't understand Diesel without talking to someone."[353]

"At Diesel, they're ensuring that there's some level of theater on the floor that they have control over," said Paco Underhill, the author of *Why We Buy: The Science of Shopping*. "They own the set and one of the actors who can drive the interaction."[354]

Roots in Rabbits and Rock 'n' Roll

Rosso's creation of the money of mayhem emerged from similarly chaotic roots. He initially tried various moneymaking schemes—"from breeding rabbits to playing rock guitar."[355] Then, in 1970, Rosso enrolled in a clothing production course at his local technical institute. "I had to do something," he recalls. "And it seemed as good a choice as anything else." Three years later, he launched "Diesel," so named "because it's one of the few words pronounced the same in every language," Rosso explained.[356] Some people pronounce it Diesel. Others deranged. Rosso can call it chaos cha-ching.

CHAPTER 18 **The Recipe for a Guerrilla Campaign**

The Chairman speaks:

"What we've got here, Mr. McIlroy, amounts to the '*Good Housekeeping* Seal of Approval' for your product . . . the 'Intel Inside . . .'"

MAO

The Recipe for a Guerrilla Campaign

 Both in its development and in its method of application, guerrilla warfare has certain distinctive characteristics. . . . There are certain fundamental steps necessary in the realization of this policy, to wit:

1. Arousing and organizing the people
2. Achieving internal unification politically
3. Establishing bases
4. Equipping forces
5. Recovering national strength
6. Destroying enemy's national strength
7. Regaining lost territories

—Mao Tse-tung

The Recipe for a Guerrilla Campaign

Mao's seven ingredients for a guerrilla campaign translate into specific actions in the boardroom:

1. *Arousing and organizing the people*: The masses are the troops of the guerrilla campaign. Without them, the campaign is nothing.

2. *Achieving internal unification politically*: Only with internal harmony can the guerrilla campaign wreak disharmony on the competition.

3. *Establishing bases*: The campaign must have a safe haven. It must have pieces of the competitive landscape that it can carve out and claim as its own.

4. *Equipping forces*: The campaign must have an army with adequate tools at its disposal to carry out attacks.

5. *Recovering national strength*: With adequate resources, the

IN THE
BOARDROOM

campaign can take over previously unexplored elements of the market.

6. *Destroying enemy's national strength*: With adequate resources, the campaign can undermine elements of the market owned by the competition.

7. *Regaining lost territories*: With adequate resources, the campaign can undermine elements of the market owned by the competition—elements we once owned ourselves.

Rules 1 through 7 are integral elements of **Nike**'s and **Ian Schrager**'s playbooks. They have used these ingredients to cook up guerrilla campaigns to near perfection.

Their Rules: One competition or another— it's all the same.

Our Rules: Nothing compares to the taste of a home-cooked revolution.

Nike's Formula of Blood, Sweat and Waffle Irons

Nike hasn't always been the Goliath of the sneaker business. "We were the children of Holden Caulfield," says cofounder and CEO Phil Knight. "Nobody liked the phoniness or the hypocrisy of the establishment, including the business establishment."

Nike's roots are about as unphony as they come: The year was 1964, and Knight and his former track coach William Bowerman each pooled together five hundred dollars to make a better running shoe. They called the company "Nike," after the Greek winged goddess of victory. They paid a local design student at Portland State thirty-five dollars to develop the swoosh logo. And then Bowerman serendipitously discovered Nike's patented textured sole: "I was looking at my wife's waffle iron," recalls Bowerman, "and I thought it looked like a pretty good traction device."[357]

People, Not Products

Nike's early successes against Goliaths Adidas and Puma came through Knight's simple but critical realization: "People don't root for a product . . . but for a favorite team or a courageous athlete." In 1973,

Nike bucked the industry standard of under-the-table handouts and began sponsoring athletes—most notably, star runner Steve Prefontaine.[358]

At that time, Nike was racking up sales of about $3.2 million.[359] By the year 2002, the company was bringing in nearly $10 billion.[360] That's a heck of a lot of sneakers.

The Guerrilla Olympics

Nike's rise to business dominance came as a result of forcing industry leaders to play by its upstart guerrilla rules. For example, in the 1996 Olympics, Nike didn't play the conventional competitor game by forking over $40 million to lay claim as an official

> **Nike's early successes against Goliaths Adidas and Puma came through Knight's simple but critical realization: "People don't root for a product . . . but for a favorite team or a courageous athlete."**

sponsor. To the innocent bystander, it would have been hard to tell.

It's true, Nike wasn't allowed to put the five magical rings on its products, but it did sponsor hundreds of individual athletes and teams, who, in turn, sported the swoosh on their uniforms and shoes. And Nike did convert a four-story parking garage into "Nike Park"—a veritable Nike extravaganza just outside Centennial Olympic Park, where most of the official sponsors were stuck inside cramped booths. Of course, Nike also spent $30 million for advertising for the event. Again, unless your glasses had a pretty strong prescription, it was hard to tell the difference between Nike and the other "official" sponsors.[361]

Much of the unprecedented $30 million in Nike's advertising went toward a campaign that effectively stole the thunder of competitor Reebok. Reebok was on the verge of out-Nikeing Nike with a hard-core image and hard-core athletes.

So what did Nike do? It re-Niked itself with the "Search and Destroy" television campaign that declared: "You don't win silver, you lose gold."[362] The ads portrayed "Olympic athletes as full-fledged warriors, kicking, jumping, falling—whatever it takes for victory—all framed by a crescendo of punk rock music. The spot ended with a runner vomiting violently and a bloody mouthpiece sailing across an image of the Nike logo. Very in-your-face." Dan Wieden of Nike's ad agency Wieden & Kennedy described "Search and Destroy" as an effort to "rip away at the Mary Poppins aspect of the Olympics."[363]

Anti-Advertising Advertisements

Looking back on Nike's guerrilla success, one cannot discount the importance of Dan Wieden and Wieden & Kennedy. They were the megaphone filter through which Nike's propaganda would pass. In 1982, when Knight first introduced himself to Wieden at his tiny Portland, Oregon agency, Wieden was greeted with, "Hi, I'm Phil Knight, and I hate advertising." Wieden responded that he "hated most advertising himself."[364]

"We don't set out to make ads," explains Wieden. "The ultimate goal is to make a connection."[365]

Knight, Nike and Wieden have connected with the masses consistently over the past four decades. Today, Nike is looking to re-Nike itself yet again by expanding its already expansive market beyond those who have traditionally been described as "athletes."

Nike is ditching its original mission "To be the world's best sports and fitness company." The new

Mao was there.

Mao and Nike's Phil Knight pictured in front of a Michael Jordan poster. "Phil wanted to call them 'Michael's Sneakers,'" Mao recalls. "But I said, 'Why don't you try "Air Jordans"? It has a better ring to it.'"

credo is "To bring inspiration and innovation to every athlete[*] in the world." The asterisk denotes a quote from founder Bill Bowerman: "If you have a body, you are an athlete."[366]

Given the omnipresence of the swoosh, it might appear as though Nike has already brought its product to every human on planet Earth who has a body. But in true guerrilla fashion, Nike isn't afraid to once again return to the power of the masses to continue its movement. Just (continue to) Do It.

Ian Schrager Delivers Studio 54 via Room Service

Ian Schrager and his boyhood friend Steve Rubell revolutionized the 1970s out of Studio 54, their cultural headquarters. In the 1990s and beyond, Schrager teamed up with "France's dauphin of design,"[367] Philippe Starck, to revolutionize the hotel business.

Studio 54 redefined nightclubs. It made waiting in line to get in a part of the event. It brought pomp and circumstance to disco. Two decades later, Schrager redefined hotels—transforming lobbies into nightclubs, rooms into experiences.

Selling an Experience

"I'm more of a social scientist than a businessman or a hotelier," explains Schrager. "When I sit down with Philippe, we talk about the sociology: What are people doing, what are they avoiding, where are people going, where are they moving—together, en masse, or apart? We're not talking about fabrics or walls or design, but the whole idea of the way people behave."[368]

If Schrager is a social scientist, then Studio 54 was most certainly his laboratory. One simple, yet important finding that emerged from the Studio 54 labs was the importance of the club as a venue both to see and be seen—something that had been missing from the traditional, reclusive hotel environment.

"We try to make people want to come and see our hotels," says Schrager. "We as a species never lose

> **Studio 54 redefined nightclubs. Two decades later, Schrager redefined hotels—transforming lobbies into nightclubs, rooms into experiences.**

our desire to be part of what's going on, and that's what I try to sell."[369]

"Ian has managed to transfer some of that mysterious glamour he brought to his nightclubs," says Anthony Haden-Guest, author of *The Last Party,* a book about Studio 54.[370] Schrager says that a core element of the Studio 54 legacy was to "create magic, to give people a dynamic ambience, a point of departure."[371] Magic, ambience and departure saturate the Schrager hotel experience.

Lobbying for Success

Much of Schrager's hotel dynamism comes from the lobby. What had previously been understood by the industry as a conduit area in between the entrance and the guest's room suddenly became a venue for visibility and enjoyment. "Hotels are not

> **Much of Schrager's hotel dynamism comes from the lobby. What had previously been a conduit area in between the entrance and the guest's room suddenly became a venue for visibility and enjoyment.**

just places to sleep," Schrager says. "You're supposed to have fun there."[372] "Here," Philippe Starck adds, "everyone gets to be famous for their fifteen seconds."[373]

In Manhattan, the lobby of Schrager's Royalton Hotel runs an entire indoor city block, providing guests with their own private fashion runway (or landing strip if need be). *Vogue* once called the

Mao was there.

Mao and Ian Schrager inside Studio 54. The Chairman is visibly irritated after having waited behind the velvet rope for three and a half hours to get in.

Delano in Miami Beach "America's coolest hotel." It boasts the nation's first indoor/outdoor lobby, creating "the feeling of an interwoven 'village' with almost no separation between indoors and out." The Mondrian Hotel in Los Angeles greets guests with "diaphanous curtains, glowing glass walls and eclectic furnishings," prompting *House and Garden* to deem it "the quintessence of cool."[374]

Despite the fact that the staff at Schrager's establishments are "famously even better-looking than the clientele,"[375] guests receive more than their fair share of stardom. Part of the Schrager experience entails that by simply being there, you are a star. Schrager explains, "When I started up, I wanted to know why we should stay in the same kind of hotels our parents did when we didn't dress the same or act the same or eat the same. My hotels are for people who want to stand out from the crowd and do their own thing."[376]

At Schrager's hotels in New York, Miami, San Francisco, Los Angeles and London, people have been standing out and doing their own thing—in droves—just as they did at Studio 54. "People expected to see go-go dancers in the lobby," cracks Schrager.[377] Always the social scientist, Schrager has understood that even without the disco, the dance is alive and well.

CHAPTER 19 **Guerrilla Warfare Still Means Leading Clean**

The Chairman speaks:

"But if we just take our employee options off the books, our profits go up from there to THERE!"

MAO

Guerrilla Warfare Still Means Leading Clean

> The idea that officers can physically beat or severely tongue-lash their men is a feudal one and is not in accord with the conception of self-imposed discipline. Discipline of the feudal type will destroy internal unity and fighting strength.
>
> —Mao Tse-tung

Guerrilla Warfare Still Means
Leading Clean

We wreak havoc on the competition, not on our troops. We bring disharmony on the competition by cultivating harmony within our forces. We lead with honor and dignity to earn the respect of our following.

Their Rules: Our troops are only a means to the end of owning the marketplace.

Our Rules: Our troops cannot be forsaken; they must be with us at the end when we own the marketplace.

Yvon Chouinard has transformed his outdoor apparel company **Patagonia** into one of the cleanest operators around. It is often said that dung rolls downhill. Given Chouinard's leadership style, apparently "clean" does as well.

IN THE
BOARDROOM

Patagonia's Yvon Chouinard Leads a Dirtbag Crusade of Cleanliness

Yvon Chouinard, the founder and majority owner of the outdoor apparel company, Patagonia, Inc., has taken "leading clean" to new heights. One of the keys to his clean strategy is by hiring "filthy" employees: "We need to seek out and hire dirtbags," says Chouinard (pronounced shuh-NARD). "These are the passionate outdoors people who are our core customers. We believe that it is easier to teach these people business than to turn the businessman into a passionate outdoor person."[378]

Let Dirtbags Reign

Dirtbag culture at Patagonia is quite pervasive: The dude who answers the phone is an eleven-time world champion freestyle Frisbee player. One of Patagonia's vice presidents grows organic produce to sell at farmers' markets. "Patagoniacs are an eclectic bunch," explains the company Web site. "Some would say quirky. Others, less understanding, might say wacky."[379]

Patagonia is consistently named one of the nation's "top 100" places to work—a product of its fair and fun atmosphere.[380] Work spaces are communal.

Business cards have no titles. There is a volleyball court out back, and showers in the rest rooms.[381] "We may not offer on-site dry cleaning like some companies," states a Patagonia brochure, "but who needs it when you get to wear shorts and T-shirts to work."[382]

"When the surf's up, you go surfing," says Chouinard, a lifelong outdoorsman and admitted "dirtbag" himself. "Why should you care about what hours your employees work as long as the work gets done?"[383]

It should be noted that the work has been getting done—to the tune of over $250 million in sales in 2001.[384]

Clean Outside and In

Leading clean has been a core element of Patagonia's success. And leading clean has meant leading clean inside the company and outside.

Internally, in addition to the numerous perks—such as on-site daycare and the opportunity for employees to take a paid leave of up to two months to work for a nonprofit group of their choice[385]—Patagonia has been a leader in ensuring a nonhierarchical, fair workplace.

Women hold more than half of Patagonia's top-paying jobs (the top 20 percent of the pay range) and nearly 60 percent of managerial jobs. And five of the eight directors are women. Women account for 52.7 percent of the workforce.[386]

This comes at a time when only about 5 percent of senior managers at the largest corporations are

> "You can't ever let up," insists Patagonia's Chouinard. "You have to foment revolution. Patagonia's ... an attempt to prove that being ecologically responsible works. And every time we've done the right thing, it's ended up making us more money."

women, and ninety-six of the top five hundred companies have no women on their boards.

Terri Wolfe, Patagonia's human resources director, said that just 4.5 percent of Patagonia's seven hundred workers leave in a typical year, compared with 25 percent at some rivals.[387]

Kris McDivitt Tompkins, who spent twenty years

with Patagonia, until she resigned as chief executive in 1993, explains the company's cooperative climate, "We have a joke that begins, 'How many Patagonia employees does it take to change a lightbulb?' The answer she continues, "Sixteen. Four to learn everything there is to know about filament technology, two to design a special pair of gloves that are perfect for lightbulb changing, and . . . "[388]

Another element of Patagonia's internal fairness is an environment of transparency. After the company had a round of layoffs in 1991, the books were opened to employees to show them why expenses needed to be reined in.[389] Now, over a decade later, this transparency continues. Even the most-junior retail-store salespeople are briefed on the company's financial performance.

Spreading Clean Throughout the Land

Patagonia's internal cleanness is only one part of the equation. It's the company's external purity that has made Patagonia synonymous with eco-friendly. After the 1991 restructuring, Chouinard emerged with a new mission: "He would change American business by using Patagonia as a model of 'sustainable industry,' one that neither harms the environment nor grows so quickly that its own viability is jeopardized."[390]

Patagonia would later trailblaze the manufacturing of shirts and pants with organic cotton, and jackets with material spun from recycled plastic bottles. Chouinard would also impose a 1 percent "Earth tax" on Patagonia,[391] generating more than a million dollars for eco-groups that might otherwise receive no funding at all.[392]

"Chouinard's not financially driven," says Bill Bussiere, a former Patagonia CFO. "He just doesn't give a shit. He and [wife] Malinda could make millions if they went public, but they don't want to. Yvon feels he could be a better instrument of change if he keeps things in his own hands. His main concern is to be a force."[393]

"You can't ever let up," Chouinard insists. "You have to foment revolution. Patagonia's an experiment, really, an attempt to prove that being ecologically responsible works. And every time we've done the right thing, it's ended up making us more money."[394]

No Bullshit

Chouinard isn't afraid to take his straight-shooter attitude outside the boardroom. NBC newscaster and friend Tom Brokaw recalls an outing with Chouinard on the Kautz Glacier in Washington, "We were [crossing] this very treacherous stretch of black ice, and if you slipped, it was at least two thousand feet before you'd stop. So I turned to Yvon and said, 'Shouldn't we rope up together here?' And he said, 'No way! If you go, I go!' He said, 'This is just like getting a taxi in New York! It's every man for himself!' There's no bull-

Mao was there.

Mao pictured with Patagonia's Yvon Chouinard on one of their many treks. Mao lamented, "If only they had had polar fleece in my day!"

shit factor when you're with him. With Chouinard, you can either do it, or you can't. And I live in a bullshit world," Brokaw says, laughing, "so it's a perfect antidote to that."[395]

> **"There's no bullshit factor when you're with [Chouinard],"** says friend Tom Brokaw. **"And I live in a bullshit world."**

"It's Brokaw's stories that have kept me from similar adventures," says Chouinard's Jackson, Wyoming neighbor Harrison Ford. "I've gone fishing with Yvon and I've played tennis with him," says the actor, "but I have not gone up a mountain with [him]. I don't trust Yvon to know the limits of a natural human being."[396]

While Chouinard may not understand the limits of a natural human being, he has understood and pushed the limits of a natural company—by leading clean inside and out.

CHAPTER 20 **Guerrilla Warfare Still Means Fighting Clean**

The Chairman speaks:

"Kids these days . . . don't even know the basics of off-balance-sheet accounting!"

MAO

Guerrilla Warfare Still Means Fighting Clean

❝ We should study the corrupt phenomena and attempt to eradicate them....

There is also a unity of spirit that should exist between troops and local inhabitants . . . put into practice a code known as "Three Rules and the Eight Remarks," which we list here:

RULES	REMARKS
All actions are subject to command.	*Be courteous.*
Do not steal from the people.	*Be honest in your transactions.*
Be neither selfish nor unjust.	*Return what you borrow.*
	Replace what you break.
	Do not without authority search those you arrest.
	Roll up the bedding on which you have slept.
	Do not bathe in the presence of women.
	Replace the door when you leave the house.

We further our mission of destroying the enemy by . . . treating his captured soldiers with consideration, and by caring for those of his wounded who fall into our hands.

—Mao Tse-tung

Guerrilla Warfare Still Means Fighting Clean

Some people make the mistake of using the term "guerrilla" as a euphemism for "dirty." When people lie, steal and cheat their ways to financial success, some say they are shrewd, cunning or "guerrilla."

This couldn't be farther from the truth.

Being a guerrilla entails using cunning and intelligent strategy within the framework of honesty and integrity.

Their Rules: When people lie, steal and cheat their way to financial success, they are guerrillas.

Our Rules: When people lie, steal and cheat their way to financial success, they are liars, thieves and cheaters— nothing more.

Anita Roddick has taken **The Body Shop** to new heights of hygienic fighting. Her style is so pure, so spotless, she might as well be called "Mrs. Clean."

IN THE BOARDROOM

The Body Shop's Anita Roddick Brings Honesty, Integrity (and Aromatherapy) to the Revolution

Anita Roddick is a guerrilla who believes in fighting clean: "We have our values from the church, the temple and the mosque. Do not rob, do not murder and so on. But our behavior changes the minute we go into the corporate place; suddenly all of this is irrelevant. It is the religion of maximizing profits. I believe that business should be about public spirit, like the Quakers. It should not be about private greed."[397]

A House, Kids and Essential Oils

Roddick joined the "good fight" relatively late. In 1976, she was thirty-three years old and a mother of two young children when she and her husband Gordon opened the first Body Shop in Brighton with the help of a $6,400 bank loan. Today, The Body Shop has more than five thousand employees in over nineteen hundred stores in fifty countries across the globe.[398]

Indeed, Roddick has come a long way since the days when she sprinkled a trail of strawberry essence on the sidewalk to lure customers into her store. Or planted a newspaper article about "the morticians next door who were trying to shut her down because they thought a store called "The Body Shop' was bad for their business." Or offered products in five different sizes of containers to make her meager twenty-product line seem more robust. Or started a "refill service" positioned primarily as an eco-friendly option for cus-

> **The Body Shop's Anita Roddick has come a long way since the days when she sprinkled a trail of strawberry essence on the sidewalk to lure customers into her store.**

tomers, when it was really a way to reduce the need for new containers—which she couldn't afford.[399] Roddick explains, "Because we had no money, we had to use our brain cells. . . .We had to create theater."[400]

Roddick has certainly come a long way since those early, resourceful, theatrical days, but her core philosophy of fighting clean has remained constant throughout. The Body Shop's stated pledge is "to sell cosmetics with the minimum of hype and packaging" and "to promote health rather than glamour, reality rather than the dubious promise of instant rejuvenation."[401]

Honorable Profit

In the process of promoting reality, The Body Shop has spearheaded public protests against animal testing. It has rallied to save the whales and to stop the burning of the rain forests.[402] It has even been responsible for leading the public debate about the objectification of women in fashion. "In 1998, we produced a generously proportioned doll called Ruby that was supposed to remind people that beauty is more about confidence than thigh circumference," Roddick recalls. "The U.S. toy company Mattel threatened to sue us. It claimed Ruby was denigrating Barbie's image."[403]

Roddick has put fighting clean above everything— even above making money. "Profit is not the objective of my business," she says. "It is providing a product and a service that's good enough that people give you a profit for providing it."[404] Roddick continues, "It's making your product so glorious that . . . their reaction is, 'I love that. Can I buy that?' You want

Mao was there.

Mao and Anita Roddick fighting clean. Mao maintains his soft complexion by using The Body Shop's Shea Body Butter with SPF 15.

them to find what you are doing so wonderful that they are happy to pay your profit."[405]

Notwithstanding her ongoing celebration of fighting clean, Roddick understands that valuing the *quality* of The Body Shop's service over the *quantity* of its revenues is contrary to the core tenets of the business world. And Roddick revels in being the contrarian: "I think you can rewrite the book on business. I think you can trade ethically; be committed to social responsibility, global responsibility . . . I think you can really rewrite the book."[406]

And rewrite the book she has. The Body Shop has

been described as "arguably the most successful British enterprise of the 1980s and . . . one of the best-known global brands to this day."[407] Roddick's conviction has earned her awards, accolades and droves of adoring fans and employees. Her words of wisdom to her followers: "I want them to understand that this is no dress rehearsal. You've got one life, so just lead it. And try to be remarkable."[408] After more than a quarter-century of live performance, Anita Roddick has proven that you can be righteous, remarkable—and profitable—all at the same time.

Conclusion:
Recipe for
a Guerrilla

The Chairman speaks:

"C'mon, Abramian. I really need you to hold yours *level* with mine!"

MAO

Recipe for a Guerrilla

All guerrilla units start from nothing and grow. What methods should we select to ensure the conservation and development of our own strength and the destruction of that of the enemy? The essential requirements are . . . listed below:

- Retention of the initiative; alertness; carefully planned tactical attacks . . . tactical speed in a war strategically protracted . . .
- Conduct of operations to complement those of the regular army
- The establishment of bases
- A clear understanding of the relationship that exists between the attack and the defense
- The development of mobile operations
- Correct command

The enemy, though numerically weak, is strong in the quality of his troops and their equipment; we, on the other hand, are strong numerically but weak as to quality. These considerations have been taken into account in the development of . . . a war that, strategically speaking, is defensive in character [and] protracted in nature. Our strategy is based on these conceptions. They must be kept in mind in the conduct of all operations. **"**

—Mao Tse-tung

Recipe for a Guerrilla

Retention of the initiative; alertness; carefully planned tactical attacks; and tactical speed.

Conduct of operations to complement those of the regular army.

The establishment of bases.

A clear understanding of the relationship that exists between the attack and the defense.

The development of mobile operations.

Correct command.

Next to each of these ingredients are the names Hayek, Ulrich, Kanbar, Kelleher, Knight, Schultz, Schrager, "Franchise," Fanning, Bezos, Branson, Ben, Jerry, Jobs, Roddick, Rosso, Rowland, Grove, Ghosn, Jung, Jannard, Chouinard, Mohajer, McCourt, McMahon, Waitt, Whitman, Winfrey, Sidney Frank and Daymond John—among many, many others.

IN THE BOARDROOM

Though they may not know it, these individuals are modern Maos. Guerrillas of our time—each with a recipe for waging effective underdog campaigns with tactical and strategic smarts.

Are you next?

¡Viva la guerrilla! The time is Mao.

Afterword

While Mao's guerrilla movement began as an earnest struggle against a nefarious oppressor, his theories have frequently been applied in suspect ways—first by himself and then by subsequent leaders.

Sowing the Seeds of Guerrilla

Mao's *On Guerrilla Warfare* was written in 1937, at a time when China was occupied by the Japanese in what became four years of terror and oppression. The Japanese occupation culminated with The Rape of Nanking in 1938—quite possibly the most brutal massacre in the history of war—in which the Japanese unsystematically and indiscriminately slaughtered more than one hundred thousand innocent civilians and committed approximately the same number of rapes.

The event was so barbaric that the Japanese military kept it a secret from the Japanese public until after the war had ended.

History Repeats Itself:
David Becomes Goliath

With the Japanese long since vanquished, Mao declared the People's Republic of China on October 1, 1949. Shortly thereafter the PRC invaded Tibet.

From 1949 to 1954, during the Cultural Revolution, Mao undertook an aggressive campaign against all

> **While Mao's guerrilla movement began as an earnest struggle against a nefarious oppressor, his theories have frequently been applied in suspect ways — first by himself and then by subsequent leaders.**

his political opponents around the country. Mao claimed to have executed some eight hundred thousand individuals described as "class enemies," but Western historians put the figure at several times that amount. He established forced-labor camps, numerous prisons and massive "re-education" and "self-criticism" programs in order to weed out counterrevolutionary political ideas.[409]

During the Chinese occupation of Tibet, six thousand Tibetan monasteries were destroyed, and Tibetans were forced to give up their traditional way of life; many were forced onto communal farms, where they labored away under awful conditions. Tibetan monks and nuns were required to denounce the Dalai Lama and cease their religious practice. Hundreds of thousands of Tibetans died from starvation. Hundreds of thousands more were worked to death, or tortured, or executed outright.

The International Commission of Jurists has labeled the situation in Tibet a genocide.[410]

Where was Mao?

A Chinese man stands alone to block a line of tanks on Beijing's Cangan Boulevard in Tiananmen Square on June 5, 1989. The name "Tiananmen" means "Gate of Heavenly Peace." In recent years, China has lost sight of the roots of freedom and liberty upon which it was built and has become similar to the oppressors against which Mao originally revolted.

Part of the author's profit from the sale of each copy of this book is donated to the Milarepa Fund. The Milarepa Fund is an international organization that supports the Tibetan people's nonviolent struggle to regain their freedom.

For more information and to access the endnotes cited in this book, go to:

www.maointheboardroom.com

Acknowledgments

I would like to thank my incredibly loving family and friends for their patience and support while I disappeared into my own private trenches writing (and sometimes fighting) this book. I would also like to thank my editor, Comrade Elizabeth Beier, for her unending commitment to the movement. Finally, Mao tells us that "Because guerrilla warfare basically derives from the masses and is supported by them, it can neither exist nor flourish if it separates itself from their sympathies and cooperation." Accordingly, I would like to thank the masses of my hometown/guerrilla enclave in Mendocino, California. You taught me from an early age what it means to be revolutionary.

About the Author

PHOTO BY LUIS GUERRA, JR.

Gabriel Stricker is a New York–based management consultant who specializes in communications. He has worked on guerrilla communications campaigns for companies and political candidates throughout the world—from American Airlines and Agilent Technologies to the presidents of Kazakstan and Colombia.

Stricker has lectured on political research and corporate branding and positioning for Columbia University, the University of California at Los Angeles and the International Diplomacy Council, and has provided political and economic commentary on Fox News and MSNBC.

He received his undergraduate degree from the University of California at Berkeley and his master's degree in International Affairs from Columbia University, with a concentration in International Commerce and Trade.

In need of some
Mao in *your* boardroom?

For more information about one-day seminars with Gabriel Stricker on how guerrilla marketing can revolutionize your organization, log on to www.maointheboardroom.com